Table of Contents

Governing Against Freedom

Our Constitution Under Siege

by

Jacob Clifton

Governing Against Freedom: Our Constitution Under Siege

"The people are the only legitimate fountain of power"
- James Madison

Contents

Introduction

Liberty and justice. These aren't just words; they're the bedrock of a promise—the promise of a nation that holds individual rights as sacred and irrevocable. Yet, that promise is under threat. A reality looms beneath the surface, where the freedoms engraved into our Constitution are slowly being chiseled away. This book is a wake-up call, a siren in the calm night, alerting us to the subtle cracks forming in the foundation of our liberties.

At every turn, history has shown us how easily power can expand, encroaching upon the private lives and rights of citizens. Today, we stand at a crucial juncture where the vault of our freedoms seems increasingly unlocked by those who were elected to guard it. Our Constitution—our parchment barrier—is being interpreted in ways that could be argued betray the trust of its framers. It's here and now that we must ask ourselves: Is our Constitution merely an artifact of a bygone era, or is it a living testament to a set of timeless principles?

The evolution of government reach, with its complex interplay between the legislative, judicial, and executive branches, has far surpassed the simple mechanisms outlined by the nation's founders. While the Constitution was crafted to ensure a balanced and fair governance, today's reality begs us to question if we've strayed too far from its intended path.

In this domain of civil discourse and critical examination, the stakes couldn't be higher. The erosion of constitutional rights doesn't just alter legal precedents; it permeates the fabric of our everyday lives, reshaping our society's character. If left unchecked, we might wake up in a world where our voices are stifled, and our autonomy is but a concept confined to history books.

Our exploration begins in the shadow of the very symbol of freedom—the Statue of Liberty—as we delve into the rise of government overreach and its implications, examining how each crack appeared and widened over time. We decode the Constitution, not as legal scholars, but as engaged citizens, determined to understand the very document that is meant to protect us. As we unpack the amendments, we reveal not just their legalese but their soul—the spirit that animates them in our modern world.

The threats to free speech have never been more nuanced, stretching the fabric of the First Amendment to the brink. In our quest for security, the Second Amendment faces its own set of battles, igniting cultural wars over the personal right to bear arms. Likewise, the Third and Fourth Amendments remind us of the sanctity of privacy and property, underscoring the risks of a burgeoning surveillance state and the controversies of eminent domain.

The Fifth and Sixth Amendments cast a stark light on how the rights of the accused are upheld, or in troubling cases, dismissed. The principles of due process and fair trials stand as guardians against tyranny, yet they are often overshadowed by the urgency of law and order.

Civil liberties, particularly those assured by the Seventh and Eighth Amendments, face assaults from within the justice system itself. Our discussions will navigate these waters, scrutinizing how the noble intention of safeguarding individual rights balances against society's quest for justice and security.

The saga continues with the Ninth and Tenth Amendments, the so-called "forgotten guarantees," exploring the tension between states' powers and federal overreach. The trident of governance—the executive, judicial, and legislative branches—each push the limits, testing the elasticity of executive orders, judicial interpretations, and legislative maneuvers.

As we journey through the chapters, analyzing the latter amendments and their embodiment in contemporary America, the aim is not merely academic. This discourse is meant to ignite a spark—empowering us to recognize when encroachments occur, and more critically, to be equipped with the knowledge to challenge them.

The grand finale of our exploration isn't just an end but a beginning—a battle cry for citizens to arise and zealously reclaim the reins of constitutional governance. Civic engagement, education, and grassroots movements aren't suggestions; they are imperatives for the enduring vitality of our republic.

So embark on this endeavor not just as a reader, but as a guardian of the ideal that "We the People" truly means something. That it always has. That it must. Here, we stand on the precipice of change, armed with the most potent weapons in our democratic arsenal—awareness and determination. It's time to reaffirm the core of what it means to be American and ensure that the lights of liberty and justice do not dim on our watch. This mission doesn't just belong to the learned legal scholars, the impassioned activists, or the stalwart policymakers—it belongs to us

all. Together, let's mend the cracks and fortify the pillar
that has long held our nation high: the Constitution of the
United States of America.

Chapter 1: In the Shadow of Liberty: The Rise of Government Overreach

Since the cherished dawn of America, liberty has been the unyielding pillar upholding the dreams and aspirations of a nation. Yet, we find ourselves wrestling with an unsettling reality; the beacon of freedom is now clouded by the growing specter of government overreach. As citizens vested in the pursuit of our inherent rights, we need to comb through our history, identifying the moments when the scales tipped—gradually, at first, then with undeniable haste. This chapter maps out the concentric circles of influence and control that expand far beyond what the framers of the Constitution intended. The promise of our democracy, the very freedoms we exalt, are not just under siege—they're incrementally being chiseled away by legislation and actions that many have missed in the din of daily life. Here, now, we stand in the shadow of Liberty herself, tasked with the sobering charge to cast light on the obscured paths where our government has overstepped its bounds. This is not merely an academic exercise but a call to arm ourselves with knowledge, awareness, and the audacity to question—and when necessary, to challenge—the encroachments that threaten to undermine the foundation upon which this country was built. The journey begins at the historical crossroads of intentions and consequences, propelled by a mandate to safeguard our future in a fortress of vigilance fortified by the past.

Historical Perspectives Unlocking the narrative of government overreach requires a deep dive into history, where the delicate balance between liberty and security has perpetually teetered. At the nation's inception, the founders crafted a constitution designed as armor against the onslaught of government power, a reflection of the hard-won lessons from their struggle against a distant monarchy. However, with time's passage, the brilliance of these protections has been dulled by actions taken in the name of necessity, often amidst the fervor of conflict or perceived threats.

The tale is as old as the republic itself, with the Alien and Sedition Acts of 1798 serving as an early testament. These laws, passed in a climate of uncertainty and fear of foreign influence, targeted immigrants and curtailed the freedom of speech. The controversy they sparked highlighted a foundational challenge: defending national security while preserving individual rights. It is in such moments of perceived peril that the constitutional compass has often been neglected, with consequences that echo through the ages.

Moving into the 19th century, the cataclysm of the Civil War tested the bounds of executive authority. The suspension of habeas corpus by President Lincoln, although deemed a wartime necessity, raised questions about the lengths to which the government could go in suppressing dissent and curtailing liberties. These actions, taken in the cauldron of internal conflict, remind us that the struggle between security and freedom is not merely philosophical but also painfully practical.

The World Wars brought forth new challenges, with the Espionage Act of 1917 and the subsequent Sedition Act of

1918 restricting speech deemed harmful to the war effort. However, they sowed the seeds of modern debates about the scope of government power and the limitations on speech and privacy. The internment of Japanese Americans during World War II remains an indelible scar on the nation's conscience, a stinging example of rights abridged under the shadow of fear and prejudice.

The Cold War era witnessed similar tensions, with anti-communism fervor leading to actions that infringed upon civil liberties. The McCarthy hearings and the activities of the House Un-American Activities Committee during the 1950s are emblematic of this era's overreach, where the right to free association and privacy were subverted by an invasive hunt for "un-American" activities.

The 1960s and 1970s unveiled new frontiers of government intrusion, particularly the revelation of wiretapping and surveillance by entities like the FBI and CIA. It was the Watergate scandal, however, that pushed public trust to the brink and reaffirmed the necessity of holding power to account. The resulting reforms sought to rein in the unchecked surveillance and covert activities that had become all too commonplace.

In the latter part of the twentieth century and the dawn of the twenty-first, technological advances revolutionized surveillance capabilities, raising novel questions about privacy. The challenge of balancing safety with freedom became ever more complex as the digital realm opened new avenues for both communication and monitoring. The capacity for government watchfulness grew exponentially, stirring debates on the Fourth Amendment's relevance in a digital age.

The September 11th attacks in 2001 marked a turning point, propelling the United States into a new era of security measures. The ensuing Patriot Act would reach into every corner of American life, expanding government surveillance powers and provoking contentious discussions about the trade-offs between individual rights and communal safety. This act epitomizes the historical cycle of reaction and overreach in times of crisis, fueling conversations about oversight and the limits of authority.

Reflecting on these patterns, it becomes clear that the struggle to maintain a constitutional equilibrium is an enduring one. Each era brings its own challenges, and with them, the temptation for government to step beyond its bounds. Yet, this historical perspective serves not to dishearten but to galvanize. Understanding the cyclical nature of overreach empowers citizens to remain vigilant, to question, and to demand accountability.

The examination of the past elucidates the path forward. Liberty, once relinquished, is lamentably arduous to reclaim. Acknowledging the transgressions against constitutional rights that history presents, equips society with the wisdom to foresee and forestall similar encroachments in the present and future.

In confronting these historical examples, a common thread emerges: the presumption that safety requires the sacrifice of freedom is a flawed axiom. Time and again, the restoration of rights and the recalibration of government power have followed the recognition that both security and liberty are not only desirable but indispensable for a flourishing republic.

This chronicle of overreach, viewed through the lens of history, reinforces the conviction that individual rights are the bedrock upon which a just and stable nation is built. As champions of liberty, citizens must wield the lessons of the past as a beacon to guide their vigilance, lest the shadows of complacency invite the repetition of history's missteps.

As this section concludes, remember history is not merely a record of past events—it is the reservoir of the nation's collective wisdom. It is incumbent upon every generation to drink deeply from this well, to comprehend the complexities of government power, and to remain steadfast in the pursuit of a more perfect union where rights are not mere parchment promises but the living reality for all.

The onus is upon us, inheritors of a legacy of liberty, to preserve the integrity of the Constitution. It is a mantle passed from one generation to the next, a perpetual call to action to sustain the balance between order and freedom. It is herein that the essence of the republic resides, and where the power for constitutional governance must ultimately be secured—by the informed, engaged, and resolute citizenry. This is not merely civic duty; it is the bedrock of our identity as a nation. On this charge rests the future of our republic.

The Patriot Act and Its Implications In the narrative of American freedom versus security, few legislative acts loom as large as the USA PATRIOT Act. In the wake of the September 11th attacks, this legislation ushered in new norms under the guise of national security, profoundly affecting the relationship between individuals and their government.

Consider the time post-9/11—a nation reeling, fear a palpable thread weaving through the fabric of society. The Patriot Act emerged as a swift response. Overnight, it shifted the paradigm, raising the question—where does one's right to privacy end and the need for national security begin?

Through the Patriot Act, substantial powers were granted to law enforcement and intelligence agencies. Some may argue that these measures are necessary tools. However, it's crucial to assess the impact on liberties viewed as inalienable before this legal pivot.

Surveillance, once an action reserved for high-standard criminal investigations, became ubiquitous. The Foreign Intelligence Surveillance Act (FISA), existing since 1978, expanded in scope, reducing the barrier for authorities to monitor communications of U.S. citizens.

Library records, internet browsing histories, and other personal data became accessible without the need for a traditional warrant. The standard of 'probable cause' was supplanted by 'relevant to an investigation,' a conspicuously vague criterion. We've witnessed a shift from targeted surveillance to wholesale data collection, inadvertently ensnaring innocent citizens in an intelligence net cast far too wide.

Section 215 and the subsequent metadata collection program underscore this broadening surveillance. This change raised an alarm. Does this unchecked scrutiny align with the Fourth Amendment's protection against unreasonable searches?

Beyond surveillance, the Patriot Act also impacted financial privacy. The act bolstered the government's ability to scrutinize financial transactions, ostensibly to thwart funding for terrorist activities. However, its implementation has brokered a significant amount of financial oversight into the hands of the state.

Material support statutes within the Act present another challenge. Persons providing 'material support' could face charges without intent or knowledge of supporting terrorism. This extends the boundaries of culpability to a degree that tests the essence of men's real fundamental principle that considers the intent behind a criminal act.

Detention policies, as well, intensified under the Patriot Act. Notably, immigrants faced detentions and deportations with lower evidentiary standards. The Act seemingly endorses a 'guilty until proven innocent' approach, conflicting with the core constitutional principle of 'innocent until proven guilty.'

National Security Letters (NSLs), a form of subpoena for communication records, gained infamy for their expansive use. Accompanied by gag orders, they prevent open discussion about such directives. This opacity contrasts starkly with the concept of transparent governance and due process.

Resistance to this act is not just about maintaining personal privacy; it's about preserving the integrity of a democratic society. Let's refocus our energy on the root principle that makes a democracy thrive—transparency and accountability, not just of citizens, but of the government itself.

The debate around the Patriot Act isn't merely legal; it's profoundly moral. The very foundations of democracy—the separation of powers, the checks and balances—are tested by the authorities it enshrines. When powers are tipped so heavily toward one branch, the scales of justice are no longer balanced.

Citizens must remain vigilant, asking probing questions, holding representatives accountable, and demanding that liberties not be forfeited on the altar of security. This vigilance ensures that core constitutional rights are not just remembered but are actively safeguarded.

While the Patriot Act was birthed in a time of turmoil, its lifespan and legacy continue to affect the everyday life of the ordinary American. Revisiting and re-evaluating the Act must occur within the context of both the threat model of the present and the constitutional commitments of the past.

In this informed awareness lies the power to steer the national conversation back to a balanced approach. An approach that defends against threats while deeply respecting the constitutional freedoms that define the American way of life. This commitment must be the guiding star as the nation navigates the murky waters between security and personal liberty.

Case Studies in Overreach Diving deep into the heart of government overreach, we confront a shadow that has crept across the Constitution—a shadow that threatens the very fabric of American freedom. There have been instances, stark and unsettling, where overreach has not only been suspected but flagrantly displayed. In scrutinizing these case studies, take a moment to understand that this isn't just a discussion; it's a call to recognition and action.

Consider the case of eminent domain abuse, where the seizing of private property goes beyond the intended public use interpretation. Families and small businesses have experienced firsthand the uprooting of their lives and livelihoods, not for crucial infrastructure projects, but for private developments that promise increased tax revenues. When courts side with local governments over citizens, this not only undermines the Fourth Amendment but reshapes the very notion of property rights.

The impact of the Patriot Act echoes profoundly as well. This legislation, born from the desire to protect the nation from terrorism, expanded surveillance capabilities significantly. Under the guise of security, the government's reach extended into the personal records of ordinary citizens, tapering the edge of privacy and laying groundwork for a surveillance state—a direct challenge to the Fourth Amendment's search and seizure protections.

Let's also acknowledge the reality of no-fly lists. Here, individuals can find themselves barred from air travel without clear reasons, notification, or a straightforward recourse for redress. This lack of transparency and due process is a jagged cut across the Fifth Amendment's guarantee. Lives have been disrupted, with individuals treated as guilty until proven innocent—a reversal of a foundational judicial principle.

Asset forfeiture is another arena of overreach with troubling implications. This practice involves the seizure of assets from individuals who haven't been convicted of a crime. Ostensibly used to dismantle criminal operations, it has too often resulted in the targeting of average citizens, leaving them to prove the innocence of their property without the safeguard of the presumption of innocence.

Contemplate the digital realm, where the boundaries of the First Amendment are being tested. Companies acting in concert with government directives have suppressed speech, creating a complex battleground for free expression. The encroachment here is subtle, warranting a dissection of the symbiotic relationship between corporations and government entities in regulating the digital public square.

Beyond the digital, public assembly and protest have faced excessive pushback. In various instances, law enforcement agencies have employed overwhelming force and aggressive tactics against demonstrators, chilling the right to assemble and petition the government for redress of grievances—cornerstones of democratic engagement.

Look at the prosecution of whistleblowers under the Espionage Act. Individuals who have brought to light government misconduct have faced severe consequences, signaling a stark warning to those who might follow in their footsteps—that transparency comes with a heavy cost, jeopardizing the flow of information crucial for a healthy democracy.

And consider the often overlooked Third Amendment, conjuring images of a bygone era with its assurance against quartering soldiers in private homes. Yet, its essence champions privacy and serves as a bulwark against militarization in citizen spaces. Encroachments here may not involve muskets and redcoats, but the underlying principle calls for vigilance in our age of increasing law enforcement militarization.

An exploration of the Sixth Amendment reveals instances where the right to a public trial is circumvented. Closed proceedings under the veil of national security leave defendants shrouded from public scrutiny, undermining the transparency that the justice system relies on to maintain trust and accountability.

Incarceration without charge, as seen in the aftermath of the war on terror, marked a troubling departure from due process norms. Indefinite detention in facilities like Guantanamo Bay stands as a testament to a jurisdictional gray area where the writ of the Constitution is obscured by arguments for national security, leaving detainees in a legal limbo.

The handling of the immigration crisis puts the Fourteenth Amendment's equal protection clause into question. Policies resulting in family separations and the detainment of individuals seeking asylum raise ethical and constitutional concerns, highlighting a struggle to balance the rule of law with humanity and the spirit of America as a beacon of hope.

What's more, executive actions and national emergency declarations have increasingly been used to bypass Congressional authority—raising concerns that balance the checks and balances system underpinning governmental operations are becoming skewed. Such practices set precedents stretching presidential power and challenging the framework of coequal branches of government.

The long arm of regulation demonstrates its reach when agencies craft rules that bear the weight of law without adequate oversight or public input. This administrative overreach stretches beyond the intentions of a representative democracy, positioning unelected officials as policymakers, which dilutes the power of the citizen's voice in government.

Lastly, there's the shadow cast over the Tenth Amendment, which endures as state sovereignty becomes steadily eroded by federal mandates and regulations. The delicate dance of federalism is disrupted, tipping the balance toward a centralized power that the Founders fervently argued against and the Constitution was designed to prevent.

With the evidence laid bare in these case studies, the question stands: How do we halt the overreach and safeguard the rights enshrined in the Constitution? Empowerment begins with knowledge, and so this dialogue isn't an endpoint but a starting line. The torch of liberty remains yours to bear, kindling the flame of vigilance against the encroaching shadows of overreach.

Chapter 2: Decoding the Constitution: Understanding our Founding Document

Emerging from a history of government overreach, it's essential to pivot towards the bedrock of our republic—the Constitution. This chapter is a deep dive, a meticulous study that peels back the layers of legalese to reveal the core truths and freedoms enshrined within our nation's founding document. It's a journey through each carefully crafted word and phrase designed to echo through centuries. The Constitution is not just a historical artifact, but a breathing charter that guides our daily lives. As power threatens to tip the scales away from liberty, understanding this parchment is more than an academic pursuit; it's a civic duty, a shield against tyranny, and our collective North Star. When we grasp the full spectrum of rights and restrictions the forefathers etched into every amendment, we equip ourselves with the knowledge to spot deviations and demand adherence, securing the promises etched into our national identity. It's time to unravel the complexities, to reveal the Constitution's true intent and empower every citizen to uphold its ideals, ensuring that it stands not as mere words on aged paper, but as the unwavering foundation of the Land of the Free.

Preamble and Its Promises Emerging from the shadows of past transgressions and government overreach, we pivot to a beacon of hope and aspiration—the Preamble to the United States Constitution. This foundational text isn't merely an introduction; it embodies the very essence of the nation's ideals. Setting the stage for our endeavor to understand the Constitution and its overarching goals is imperative for comprehending how modern actions measure against these foundational aspirations.

Envision the Preamble as a compass for governance, encapsulating powerful pledges to its citizens. We speak of 'We the People,' an inclusive phrase that sets democracy's tone, a collective call to action whereby every voice matters and every individual holds stake in the nation's course. It's a testament to unity, propelling us to consider the extent to which this unity holds under the weight of divisive policies and actions.

Promises of justice, tranquility, and welfare weave through the Preamble, raising a bar against which all laws and actions are to be evaluated. When policies infringe on fair practice or disturb societal peace, they fall short of these Constitutional promises. Arguably, such policies chip away at the very core of what the founders envisioned—a system equitable and serene, a sanctuary for the collective well-being of its populace.

To secure the blessings of liberty—this phrase from the Preamble resounds with a powerful echo, reminding us that freedom isn't static, but a precious commodity to be actively guarded. This isn't just about defending against visible threats, but also those insidious creeping's of power that may, under the guise of protection or efficiency, encroach upon freedoms that are core to the American ethos.

Disease grows in the shadows, and similarly, violations of Constitutional rights often brew unnoticed, only gaining attention when their symptoms can no longer be ignored. Insight into the Preamble's assurances is paramount to maintaining vigilance against such encroachments. It is the litmus test for the actions of the judiciary, the executive, and the legislature, providing a north star to guide the republic back to its Constitutional commitments when lost.

The Preamble is not merely rhetorical flourish but is infused with the intent to inspire progress. It's an acknowledgement that this great experiment in democracy is always a work in progress, striving to form a more perfect union. This continuous journey towards improvement demands an informed and active citizenry, aware of their rights and the powers granted to their government.

The Constitution is a living document, a contract between the government and its people that is as relevant today as at the time of its penning. As such, the spirit of the Preamble compels each generation to examine whether the government is honoring its charter. Scrutiny of actions and laws against these promises becomes not just a right, but a duty.

In instances where the actions of public officials, or the statutes that govern us, stand at odds with the ethos of the Preamble, a line is crossed. This calls for accountability from those in authority; a reminder that they are servants of the people, bound by the solemn words that cloak our Constitution.

The Preamble's promises beckon for justice to be served without prejudice or partiality. Any divergence from this axiom suggests a breach of the trust that underpins the justice system. It is in this light that we must view the increasing instances of prosecutorial overreach and the growth of a surveillance state as antithetical to the spirit of our founding document.

General welfare—a promise that compels policies shaping economic, social, and environmental landscapes. It is an actionable commitment that, when forgotten, fuels inequality and fosters neglect. The rise of policies that marginalize or disenfranchise counters the inclusive ethos mandated by the Preamble.

Pursuing posterity involves the safeguarding of rights not only for today's citizens but for future generations. Here, short-sighted decisions and policies have repercussions that extend beyond the temporal landscape, potentially compromising the longevity of the freedoms and protections we cherish.

Each clause in the Preamble, each pledge made, is intertwined with the liberty fibers of the nation's identity. As caretakers of this legacy, acknowledging when failures occur isn't just criticism; it is an act of patriotism, a resolute step toward reclaiming and upholding the Constitution's intent.

It is in the recognition and exercise of these sacred promises where we find the impetus for change and reformation. Only through an informed understanding of this preeminent text can a populace challenge the status quo, press for redress, and return to the Charter's original mandates when they deviate.

As we proceed, let us hold the Preamble as our guide through the labyrinth of legal, political, and social challenges that confront us. We are reminded that the answers to our modern dilemmas do not lie outside our foundational blueprint but within the heart of its promises—a declaration that has and must continue to withstand the tests of time and tyranny.

We stand at the crossroads of history, where every action against the Constitution is a seed sown in the garden of tomorrow. Through examining the Preamble and its promises, we set forth upon a path of restoration and renaissance for the core values that birthed a nation. It is here that our journey for understanding and upholding the tenets of our Constitution begins, for the sake of the present and the prosperity of the future.

A Close Look at the Bill of Rights The Bill of Rights, those first ten amendments to the U.S. Constitution, is not merely a list of ideas; it's a vital safeguard, a declaration of the citizenry's most fundamental rights. The protection of these rights is not an abstract concept; it's the lifeblood of freedom, flowing through the veins of our nation's body politic.

Let's unpack the essence of each Right. The First Amendment isn't just about freedom of speech; it's the bedrock of self-expression and a critical defense against tyranny. When voices are silenced, society stumbles toward the precipice where liberty is but a memory. This amendment also upholds the freedom of religion, assembly, press, and petition—each a pillar that, when weakened, compromises the integrity of a democratic state.

The Second Amendment protects the right to keep and bear arms, a contentious issue yet foundational for many in the realm of self-defense and as a historical buffer against oppressive governance. It symbolizes the power balance between the governed and their government, asserting the people's right to resist subjugation.

Third Amendment is often overlooked; it's a relic of a bygone era of quartering soldiers. But its spirit resonates today, representing the right to privacy in one's home and the principle that one's domicile is indeed one's castle, not to be intruded upon by the state without just cause.

The Fourth Amendment guards against unwarranted searches and seizures. Its importance cannot be overstated in a modern era teeming with surveillance—a bulwark against the all-seeing eye of an intrusive government that may seek to monitor its citizens without due process.

Turning to the Fifth Amendment, it is a sanctuary of the individual's right to due process and protects against self-incrimination, ensuring that personal liberty isn't stripped away arbitrarily. It reminds the legal system that justice is not a convenience of the state but a right of the people.

The Sixth Amendment ensures a swift and fair trial, a public forum where justice is not done in dark corners but in the daylight of public scrutiny, with the right to confront one's accusers and have legal counsel. It upholds the ideal that one is innocent until proven guilty beyond a reasonable doubt.

The Seventh Amendment's guarantee of a jury trial in civil cases over a certain amount safeguards the citizen's access to an impartial tribunal rather than the caprice of potentially biased judges, maintaining the people's grip on the legal process and stemming the overreach of judicial authority.

Meanwhile, the Eighth Amendment forbids excessive bail, fines, and cruel and unusual punishment. It is the conscience of the nation's legal system, a bulwark against the barbaric and unjust treatment that erodes the soul of a society that values human dignity and justice.

Nine and Ten, though less cited, are no less crucial. They recognize that the enumeration of certain rights does not dismiss others retained by the people, and they assert that powers not delegated to the federal government are reserved to the states or to the people. They anchor the principle of a government limited in scope and remind us of the vast domain of liberty intended to be left in the hands of the people and their more local, thus more accountable, governments.

In essence, the Bill of Rights underscores a philosophy of governance that values individual liberty to its core. It insists that certain realms of human existence are beyond the rightful reach of government. These ten amendments cast a vision of a government that serves, not subjugates; a government that protects, not preys; a government that empowers, not encroaches.

Yet, these powerful protections are not self-enforcing. They require vigilance, advocacy, and understanding from every citizen. The encroachments on these rights can be subtler than blunt force; they can creep through legislative backdoors, erode through judicial reinterpretations, and be whittled away by executive overreach. The responsibility falls upon each of us to recognize these breaches and to take a firm stand, to ensure that our rights remain intact and vibrant.

Remember, the strength of the Bill of Rights is not merely in its words but in the collective spirit it embodies. It is a challenge to complacency, a clarion call to civic vigilance, and a poetic ode to individual dignity. These ten amendments are not the ceiling of our rights but the floor upon which we stand, a starting point from which liberty expands.

Let's embrace our role as guardians of these freedoms, informed and ready to question any action that undermines these foundations. The preservation of the Bill of Rights depends not on the benevolence of authorities, but on the watchfulness and active defense by those to whom these rights belong—you, me, us.

In conclusion, the Bill of Rights isn't just a segment of our Constitution—it's a manifesto of the American experiment. It articulates a way of life worth defending, a set of principles that, when upheld, empower a nation to the greatest heights of freedom and when ignored, can signal the descent into shadows where rights are mere illusions. As custodians of a legacy of liberty, the task is ours to ensure that this national treasure, this Bill of Rights, is more than parchment, it's practiced. And that is a task both noble and necessary.

The Remaining Amendments and Their Roles As we turn our gaze beyond the Bill of Rights, we venture into the realm of amendments that have shaped the course of American history in profound ways. The later amendments are not just historical footnotes; they are vibrant and vital safeguards of our liberties, and their roles are crucial in the ongoing quest for justice and equality.

After the ratification of the Bill of Rights, the issues of governance and rights continued to evolve, leading to the need for further amendments. The subsequent amendments, starting with the 11th and ending with the 27th, address a wide range of issues from states' rights to the complexities of presidential elections, from abolishing slavery to ensuring equal voting rights for all citizens.

The 11th Amendment set the stage for sovereign immunity by limiting the ability of individuals to sue states in federal court, reflecting a balance between federal power and state integrity. This amendment, while seemingly obscure, has consistently played a role in shaping the boundaries of state and individual rights.

The 12th Amendment refined the process for electing the President and Vice President, avoiding the potential crisis created by the original system. The clarity it brought to the electoral process has safeguarded the nation's stability during the transfer of presidential power.

It took a bloody civil war to usher in the transformative 13th, 14th, and 15th Amendments, which collectively sought to redefine the nation's understanding of freedom and equality. The 13th Amendment abolished slavery, forever altering the legal landscape of American society and laying the foundational principles for civil rights.

Then came the 14th Amendment, which guaranteed equal protection under the law and due process rights to all citizens, challenges to which continue to play out across courtrooms nationwide. Its broad scope touches upon issues of discrimination, citizenship, and the protections guaranteed to individuals.

The 15th Amendment sought to prohibit discrimination in voting on the basis of race, although it would take nearly a century of struggle to see its promises fully realized.

Subsequent amendments continued to evolve our democratic processes. The 16th Amendment authorized the federal income tax, becoming a cornerstone of the modern fiscal state. The 17th Amendment changed the dynamics of representation by mandating the direct election of senators.

One of the most socially impactful changes came with the 18th Amendment, which ushered in Prohibition, only to be repealed by the 21st Amendment after a tumultuous societal experiment. These events remind us that constitutional change is not always linear and that the will of the people can overturn even established amendments.

The 19th Amendment, a triumph of the suffragette movement, granted women the right to vote, making a significant stride toward gender equality. The momentum for change continued with the 20th Amendment, which adjusted the dates for the start of presidential, vice-presidential, and congressional terms, streamlining government transitions.

The 22nd Amendment addressed the power dynamics of the presidency by limiting individuals to two terms in office, a response to the unprecedented four-term presidency of Franklin D. Roosevelt. It was a clear expression of the nation's commitment to preventing any semblance of monarchical rule.

The rights of residents in the District of Columbia were expanded by the 23rd Amendment, which granted them the right to vote in presidential elections, while the 24th Amendment outlawed the poll tax, knocking down one more barrier to voting equality.

The social upheaval of the 1960s led to the passage of the 25th Amendment, which clarified presidential succession, ensuring continuity of government leadership during the most trying of times.

More recent constitutional additions include the 26th Amendment, which lowered the voting age to 18, a recognition of the outspoken activism and maturity of the nation's youth. The 27th Amendment, regarding congressional pay adjustments, serves as a bulwark against unchecked legislator privileges.

These amendments are not mere echoes from the past; they are active players in the legal and societal arenas. They continue to influence issues that touch the core of the republic and resonate with the underlying theme of this book – the preservation and protection of constitutional rights. The amendments collectively embody the spirit of an evolving constitution, one that seeks to address present challenges while upholding the essential tenets of liberty, justice, and equality for all.

Chapter 3: First Amendment Fractures: Free Speech on the Brink

As the ink of history dries, the First Amendment remains a living testament to the power of the spoken and written word, a beacon for democracies worldwide. Yet the landscape we navigate today is riddled with unprecedented hurdles as free speech teeters on a precipice, faced with the winds of change and the tremors of modern-day challenges. This chapter is a call to action, a rallying cry for the vigilant protector of dialogue and dissent. We stand at a critical juncture, with digital platforms and governmental policies shaping the terrain upon which our most sacred right is exercised—or extinguished. It isn't merely about what we can say, but it's about the society we forge with the words we're allowed to share. Let's peel back the layers of legalese and claim our voice in the cacophony of the 21st century. What's at stake is not just a fundamental American right, but the very fabric of our democracy. Here, we confront the fractures splitting through our First Amendment right to free speech, understanding that if we don't act, who will?

Analyzing Free Speech Precedents To truly grasp the current challenges to free speech, we begin with a historical backtrack to the keystones of judicial precedent that sculpted today's landscape. The First Amendment, steadfast in its brevity, guarantees the freedom of speech—a foundational right holding the power to shape society.

In the courts, free speech has often been a battleground with varying degrees of protection. Landmark cases, such as Schenck v. United States, set the stage by introducing the "clear and present danger" test, which weighed the balance between expression and national security. The heated debate here is not simply about the bounds of expression but about the very essence of a free society.

Moving through the decades, Brandenburg v. Ohio refined the standard and enhanced speech protection by establishing the "imminent lawless action" test. This progression showcases a judicial acknowledgment of speech's central role in democracy—and any constraint here must be scrutinized intensely.

The precedence set by these cases doesn't cement free speech as untouchable but rather as a dynamic force, adaptable to the evolving fabric of time and yet consistently resilient. Every ruling, from Tinker v. Des Moines, which upheld students' rights to free expression, to Citizens United v. FEC, which controversially considered the voice of corporations, has stitched a complex tapestry of legal understanding.

Within our review, it becomes evident that precedents are not mere relics but living components of judicial reasoning. They hold the weight of past interpretations but are not impervious to the changing tides of society's values and technological advancements that disrupt traditional modes of communication and expression.

Most strikingly, the friction between society's interest in maintaining order and preserving individual empowerment emerges time and again. The courts often struggle to pinpoint the moment when vigorous debate turns into unlawful incitement—identifying this tipping point is crucial yet precarious.

Questions naturally arise about the boundaries of symbolic speech: Can a gesture, an artwork, or a silent protest convey a powerful message deserving the same shield as the written or spoken word? Through cases like Texas v. Johnson, the courts have affirmed that expression transcends the verbal, embracing diverse modes of dissent.

As we peer into this vibrant past, it is clear that the pillar of free speech is not immune to the occasional crack. Laws combating the spread of disinformation in the digital age present new challenges. These digital platforms bring forth complex questions of ownership, intent, and neutrality, taking us into uncharted territories of the First Amendment.

It becomes an intellectual imperative to recognize the subtle shifts in legal thinking which dictate the present atmosphere for speech. Through dispassionate analysis and observant vigor, understanding our rights is not just a scholarly pursuit but a democratic duty.

Moreover, as technology burgeoned, so did the arenas for free expression. Modern judicial decisions confront complexities involving social media and the internet—an entirely new frontier for free speech where precedents can only guide but not conclusively resolve new dilemmas.

The strength of these precedents lies in their ability to adapt, to reflect current social mores without losing sight of the fundamental principles upon which the First Amendment was built. In scrutinizing these historic decisions, we gain the foresight to navigate future quandaries of speech and expression.

The echo through time of past free speech rulings reminds us that while the context may evolve, the central tenets do not wane. They demand a vigilant society to vigorously assert their relevance in every era.

Indeed, the battleground of free speech does not belong to the courts alone. It extends into classrooms, workplaces, and the public squares—virtual or otherwise—where the exercise of this right tests the resilience of our constitutional fabric.

At its core, this precedence provides a lens through which we can view contemporary contentions over speech. It prompts a continual re-examination of boundaries, often underlining that the immense value of speech derives, in part, from its ability to challenge, to provoke, to innovate.

In conclusion, the precedents of free speech form a robust guard, continually interpreted by the courts with a vigilant eye toward preserving the essence of a truly unfettered discourse—a discourse that defines, defends, and develops with the vigor of the free and the brave. In understanding these milestones, citizens arm themselves with the knowledge to confront incursions on this essential liberty.

Areas of Censorship in Modern America

As we journey through the exploration of our constitutional rights, there's a pressing need to address the delicate topic of censorship—where it occurs, how it manifests, and its implications in our society. The landscape of free speech has evolved significantly with technological advancement, leading to newer domains where censorship can take root and thrive. This section scrutinizes these modern arenas, casting light on the shadows where expression is stifled.

Censorship in media has been a contentious issue for decades. Today, it's not just about what's seen on television or read in newspapers. The proliferation of digital platforms has amplified the conversation around who controls information and who decides what's accessible. In instances, tech giants have stepped into the role of gatekeepers, invoking community standards to moderate content. Concern arises when these policies are inconsistently applied or perceived to target specific viewpoints.

Even academia, a realm long cherished for promoting diverse ideas and debate, isn't exempt from censorship. Instances of speakers being disinvited from campuses or curricula being altered under pressure reflect a trend of restricting certain narratives. While the intention may sometimes be to foster a safe and inclusive environment, the effect can impede a full spectrum of discourse— crucial to the robust exchange of ideas that education thrives on.

Our fine arts reflect the pulse of society, capturing and commenting on social issues. Yet, they too face the tightening grip of censorship. When art is altered to avoid offending sensibilities or removed from public display, the cultural dialogue is diminished. Whether due to corporate interests or political pressures, the effect on creative expression and public access to diverse art forms is undeniable.

Social media has become the modern public square, where millions share their thoughts daily. However, these platforms are increasingly under scrutiny for their role in suppressing certain content. The line between curtailing harmful speech and impeding free expression is razor-thin and often contested. It's a significant concern in an era where digital communication shapes public opinion.

Government regulations, often enacted in the name of protecting citizens, can have unintentional censoring consequences. Allegations of surveillance affecting the freedom of journalists to report, or whistleblower prosecutions impacting the flow of information to the public, underscore a tension between security measures and the liberty to expose truths.

The workplace, too, serves as a battleground for expression. Companies instituting policies that limit speech can inadvertently silence discussions around important societal issues. Employees navigate a complex web of what can and cannot be said, which in some cases, can suppress discussion of workplace rights or social justice concerns.

In the wake of disasters or emergency situations, censorship has often come under the guise of public order. Information blackouts and controlling the narrative can hinder the right to access crucial knowledge. While the need for accurate, timely information is paramount, so is the need to prevent a selective flow dictated by expediency over transparency.

Libraries, the traditional bastions of knowledge, grapple with the issue of censorship through the lens of book challenges and restrictions. The tug-of-war over what literature should be accessible, particularly to young readers, has implications for educational growth and the understanding of complex issues from varied viewpoints.

The entertainment industry confronts its own form of censorship when it comes to distribution deals and content rating systems. Decisions made by a few can impact what films or shows reach audiences, potentially curbing artistic expression and dictating cultural norms.

Counterterrorism efforts have, at times, spilled over into the realm of censorship. Government monitoring and surveillance programs aimed at ensuring national security can lead to self-censorship among individuals wary of undue scrutiny, hindering the free exchange of thoughts and ideas essential in a democratic society.

Within the public sector, civil servants may face censorship in the form of gag orders or being barred from speaking on specific issues. This restriction on public employee speech can prevent valuable insights and facts from reaching the citizenry, thus narrowing the scope of public debate on policy matters.

Advertising, a powerful vehicle for conveying messages, also encounters its share of censorial influence. Corporate interests can clash with social messaging, leading to suppression of advertisement campaigns that do not align with certain commercial agendas or societal norms.

To fully cherish free speech, one must also consider the silent stranglehold of self-censorship, often the product of a charged political climate or fear of repercussions. When individuals refrain from speaking out on issues due to apprehension, the loss is twofold—their voice is stifled, and society is deprived of a potentially vital perspective.

The intersection of censorship and technology also extends to artificial intelligence, where algorithms can inadvertently or intentionally prioritize certain types of content over others. The opaqueness of these algorithms further complicates the issue, often making it difficult for users to discern why certain information is promoted or buried.

Understanding these areas of censorship is a foundational step to fostering awareness and inspiring action. To hold on to the essence of a free, expressive society, vigilance and the willingness to engage in dialogue and challenge unjust suppressions are paramount. Only then can the tenets of unfettered speech thrive, supporting the robust exchange of ideas that constitutes the nucleus of democracy.

Action Against Citizens' Voices Understanding the gravity of the situation requires a stark look at reality. Measures taken to mute the citizenry are not merely bumps in the road of democracy but rather looming chasms threatening to swallow the cornerstone of free speech. It's time to identify these threats not as isolated incidents, but as a systematic attempt to erode democratic discourse.

The First Amendment secures the right to expressive autonomy, amplifying the undercurrents of plurality and dissent that invigorate democracy. Yet, this right is increasingly hemmed in by a plethora of sly regulations, aggressive statutes, and judicial interpretations that crack the very foundation of free speech.

Censorship wears many masks. It appears in the form of 'free speech zones', a paradox that constrains the geography of protest, corralling voices to oft-ignored corners. The silence in the squares and parks, once vibrant with the nation's pulse, speaks volumes about the spaces where democracy is, and isn't, allowed to breathe.

Another guise of control is the strategic ploy of surveillance. It's the unseen watcher, chilling the willingness to vocalize opposition. It's not just the overt recording devices but the covert tapping into digital footprints that unnervingly hints: 'We're listening,' tilting the scales towards self-censorship and conformity.

We're confronted with insidious legislative efforts that seek to criminalize protest, assigning draconian penalties to civic engagement. When rallying cries for justice translate into potential prison sentences, democracy doesn't merely stumble; it falters.

Consider the plight of whistleblowers, guardians of transparency, who dare to peel back the curtain on government misdeeds. They are too often met not with commendation, but with prosecution, forced to navigate an obstacle course rigged with retribution. Their experiences embody a stark warning, whispering the cost of truth to those who dare to follow.

Amplifying platforms, specifically social media, have become fertile grounds for manipulation of narrative and suppression. Shrouded in algorithms, voices are selectively broadcasted or buried, not by the merit of their message, but by the preference of unseen, unaccountable puppeteers.

As leaders brand journalists and outlets as 'fake news', credibility becomes yet another chess piece in the strategy of suppression. It's not merely misinformation that's worrisome; it's the discrediting of legitimate dissent, stripping away the robust debate that nourishes an informed populace.

Legislation supposedly crafted to combat terror now ensnares citizen activists in its web. Laws intended to target the enemies of state are misapplied, leaving activists who challenge environmental destruction, or even animal cruelty, to face the same scrutiny as those who pose genuine threats.

Look, too, at the way grassroots movements are systematically dismantled by co-optation or by force. The machinery of power doesn't differentiate between dissenters, whether they champion social justice, fiscal responsibility, or environmental advocacy.

Academic institutions, once bastions of critical thought and revolutionary ideas, buckle under a new kind of pressure. Funding, reputation, and political favor become the noose that tightens around the neck of academic freedom, suffocating the free exchange of ideas upon which progress depends.

Under the smokescreen of securing elections, voter suppression tactics take aim at the very ethos of democracy. Gerrymandering, stringent ID laws, and reduction of polling places are not simply policy decisions; they're strategic maneuvers to quell the quintessential democratic voice — the vote.

Standing up requires courage, but what requires even more is persistence. The inexorable push for transparency, for accountability, cannot relent. Every legal challenge faced by those standing in defense of rights and freedoms isn't merely an individual battle; it's a chapter in the broader narrative of resistance.

The legal system, theoretically an avenue for justice, can become a labyrinth designed to exhaust and intimidate. Absurd bail conditions, prolonged pre-trial detentions, and overburdened public defenders create an unequal battlefield, skewing outcomes before arguments are even made.

Despite these multifaceted attempts to dilute the vigor of citizen voices, resilience emerges. It's found in community meetings, online forums, street corners, and courtrooms across the nation. The ecosystem of dissent thrives not just in the echo of chants or the vigor of marches, but in the relentless spirit that refuses to accept the status quo.

As threats to the First Amendment mount, remember the importance of vigilance. Acknowledge the power wielded by informed, engaged citizens. Stand resolute in defiance of attempts to silence. In safeguarding the freedom of expression, it's not merely personal rights that are upheld, but the very essence of democracy.

Chapter 4: Second Amendment Struggles: The Right to Bear Arms

Continuing our journey of constitutional clarity, we arrive at the Second Amendment, a contentious arena where the right to bear arms is both revered and challenged. Gun ownership in America isn't just a tradition; it is a deeply embedded legal and cultural norm, a safeguard of personal liberty, and for many, an identity's cornerstone. Yet, the simplicity of its text belies complex battles being fought in legislative halls, courtrooms, and the public square. Every day, individuals grappling with a society divided by the polarities of safety and freedom find themselves at the nexus of bearing arms and bearing witness to a changing landscape. The pages of this chapter are illuminated with stories of those who cling to the rights bestowed upon them by the framer's foresight and the efforts to place limits that some see as prudent and others perceive as transgressions. It is in understanding this struggle – the delicate dance of upholding one's rights without dismantling the collective peace – that citizens are called upon to be custodians of both their liberty and their community.

Gun Ownership: Historical Context and Current Challenges The right to bear arms is deeply embedded in the fabric of American history. Enshrined in the Second Amendment, this right has been a point of pride and a subject of intense debate across centuries. From the Minutemen of Lexington and Concord to the complexities of modern urban societies, America's relationship with gun ownership reveals a trajectory as intricate as it is controversial.

Gazing back at the citizen-soldiers of the Revolutionary era, we understand that their ability to arm themselves was integral to the birth of a nation conceived in liberty. Those early Americans saw the right to bear arms as a safeguard against tyranny, an essential tool for self-defense, and a means to fulfill civic duty in a fledgling republic.

Fast forward to the current day, and the landscape of gun ownership has metamorphosized immensely. While the Second Amendment remains a cornerstone of constitutional law, its interpretation and application have sparked polarized views, growing more contentious as challenges in society evolve.

The United States currently faces a complex matrix of issues surrounding gun ownership. Violence in urban centers, mass shootings, and the debate over assault weapons have ignited a firestorm of public discourse. Conversations spiral around the balancing act of maintaining public safety while honoring the freedoms guaranteed in the Constitution.

Advocates of stringent gun control measures argue for the necessity of adapting constitutional rights to contemporary society. They contend that reforms such as comprehensive background checks, closing loopholes at gun shows, and banning certain types of firearms could curb the instances of gun-related violence.

Contrast that stance with staunch Second Amendment proponents, who maintain that any form of gun control is a slippery slope towards the erosion of personal freedoms. They assert that responsible gun owners are unfairly targeted by restrictive laws, which do not deter criminals intent on malfeasance.

The conversation is further complicated by the varied landscape of state laws. Gun regulations differ widely from one state to another, leading to a patchwork of policies that can be a source of confusion and friction. This disparity raises questions about the federal government's role in setting coherent, nationwide standards.

Amidst this contentious debate, the judiciary continues to play a pivotal role. Courtrooms have become battlegrounds where the limits of the Second Amendment are tested and defined. Each ruling can set a precedent with far-reaching consequences for millions of Americans. The judiciary's interpretations influence policy decisions that affect the daily lives of citizens and the national conversation on rights and safety.

However, the challenge doesn't end at policy and legislation. The social fabric of the United States is frayed with instances of gun violence that impact communities across the nation. Each tragedy becomes a call to action for some, a defense rallying cry for others, as the nation grapples with how to move forward.

Likewise, the rise of modern technology adds a new dimension to the gun debate. The advent of 3D-printed guns and the spread of information on manufacturing firearms bring forth innovative considerations for regulation and law enforcement.

In the throes of these challenges, ensuring that the citizenry is well-informed remains essential. Knowledge empowers individuals to enter the dialogue on gun ownership with a clearer understanding of their rights and the implications of potential restrictions.

It's crucial to underscore the importance of participating in the legislative process. Engaged citizens can affect change, whether that involves advocating for more stringent gun laws or protecting Second Amendment rights. In a republic like ours, the voice of the people is pivotal in shaping the policies that shield our liberties and govern our society.

As we delve into the current challenges of gun ownership, we are called to reflect upon the intention behind the Second Amendment and its relevance to the lives we lead today. It is not just a matter of historical context but of continuous, active citizenship in a living, evolving democratic landscape.

Thus, the conversation about the right to bear arms cannot be a static one; it must evolve as conditions change, always with an eye on the core values of individual freedom and the collective welfare of society. Understanding our history, examining our present challenges, and actively participating in shaping the future direction of gun policy are responsibilities that each person must bear with the gravity and due respect it commands.

In the final analysis, the right to bear arms remains a defining feature of American identity. The responsibility that comes with this right is as significant today as it was at the nation's inception. How we handle the current challenges will not only define our respect for the Constitution but will lay the groundwork for the kind of society future generations will inherit.

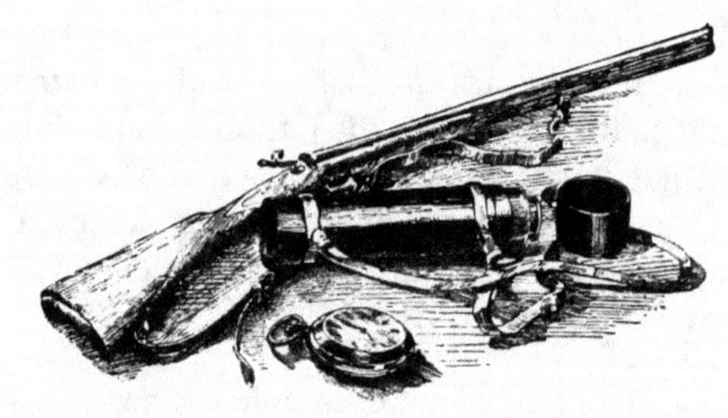

Legislative Limits and Constitutional Conflicts We're living in an era where the boundaries between legislative intent and constitutional guarantees often blur—a time when lawmakers push the envelope on restrictions that test the very framework of our founding document. In this landscape, a discerning look at the tug-of-war over the Second Amendment is not just warranted, it's crucial. Our forebears crafted a Bill of Rights with a resolution that seemed clear, yet today, interpretations of these rights ignite impassioned debates across the nation.

The Second Amendment's concise wording leaves ample room for legislative interpretation, and therein lies the seed of conflict. "A well regulated Militia, being necessary to the security of a free State, the right of the people to keep and bear Arms, shall not be infringed." The brevity and ambiguity of this statement have paved the way for a multitude of laws and regulations that often dance on the line of constitutional confines.

Laws surrounding background checks, waiting periods, assault weapons bans, magazine capacity limits, and concealed carry rights each individually and collectively test the threshold of the Second Amendment. They invite us to question: at what point do safety measures encroach upon the 'shall not be infringed' clause? There's a delicate balance to strike between preventing harm and preserving freedom, one that requires both wisdom and courage to navigate.

The battleground over gun legislation, however, isn't solely in Congress or state legislatures. It extends into the courts where constitutional interpretation becomes as powerful as the laws themselves. Legal challenges to firearm regulations bring the conflict into stark relief, as judiciary bodies measure contemporary societal needs against a centuries-old text. This is the arena where legislative limits and constitutional interpretations engage in their most decisive contests.

At the heart of these judicial skirmishes is a consideration of original intent versus living document philosophy. Does the Constitution's meaning change over time, adapting to modern circumstances, or is its original context sacrosanct, inviolate against shifting societal norms? It is in this philosophical debate that the tensions between legislative actions and constitutional fidelity most strikingly manifest.

The implications are varied and vast. Each ruling not only shapes the life of the Second Amendment but also subtly alters the canvas of the Constitution. Court cases become a patchwork that either reaffirms the Constitution's resilience or, piece by piece, alters its appearance over time. The consequences of these decisions echo beyond gun rights, influencing the manner in which we interpret every facet of America's supreme legal document.

Yet, the conflict is multi-layered, extending beyond the courtroom and into the very lives of individuals. A person's right to security via firearm ownership rubs shoulders with community safety concerns, posing moral dilemmas framed by legal constraints. This complex interplay between individual and collective rights frequently compels legislators to enact laws that are carefully designed to withstand constitutional scrutiny while aiming to prevent tragedies.

In this contemporary legal landscape, it's evident that a firm grasp on constitutional principles is not just beneficial but essential for every citizen. With lawmakers pushing boundaries and the judiciary tasked with adjudication, the ordinary citizen stands at the confluence of policy and right—a participant, willing or not, in the shaping of their constitutional reality.

As we advance into further dissections of Second Amendment challenges, we enter a realm of continuous dialogue. A dialogue that calls for engagement, for voices that demand transparency and accountability from those who shape the laws of the land. It's in this very demand where empowerment takes root, sprouting informed debate and action.

The journey through legislative limits and constitutional conflicts is a testament to the enduring spirit of the American Constitution. A spirit that withstands the test of time, debate, and judicial prudence. But more importantly, it's a reminder of the vigilant eye required to ensure that the scales of justice remain balanced in favor of the freedoms we hold dear.

There's power in understanding the interplay between legislative enactments and constitutional safeguards. Knowledge of these intricate dynamics is a shield against infringement and a beacon for those navigating the murky waters of legal interpretation. It's a call to be ever-present, ever-watchful, and unwavering in the quest to uphold the constitutional protections bequeathed to us.

So, as we reflect upon the intricacies of legislative limits against the bedrock of our Constitution, let us do so with a sense of purpose. Let us embrace the challenge of preserving the liberties defined within our founding charter while embracing the inevitability of evolution within our legal system. It's a path demanding not just passive observation, but active participation and unyielding commitment to the principles that define our national identity.

Legislative actions and constitutional rights will undoubtedly continue to be a source of contention. As long as there are rights to protect and safety to ensure, debates will rage, laws will be crafted, and court cases will be argued. Through it all, our collective understanding and resolve will dictate the future of our Constitution and the freedoms it guarantees.

One thing remains clear: the importance of steadfastly guarding the delicate equilibrium between legislative prudence and constitutional sanctity. As we dissect legislative endeavors and their constitutional impacts, let us proceed with an informed perspective, recognizing that every legal nuance contributes to the grand design of our constitutional democracy.

The Culture War Over Guns

Imagine standing at the heart of a battlefield, witnessing a clash of ideals that resonate through the essence of freedom. This is not a scenario of distant lands but a vivid portrait of America's culture war over guns. Deeply rooted in the Second Amendment of the Constitution is the foundational right to bear arms—a right that has become the lifeblood of societal debate, pitting advocates of gun rights against proponents of gun control.

Central to understanding the discourse is the historical reverence for firearms as instruments of liberty and defense. This is a legacy that transcends mere ownership, embedding itself into the national identity. Yet, contemporary challenges have produced a zeitgeist that questions the breadth and application of this right amid escalating gun violence.

Legislative battles shape the contours of this ongoing war. Each new gun control proposal brings with it a surge of resistance, amplified by fears of government overreach. The clash is not simply over the material possession of firearms but over the perceived erosion of Constitutional guarantees, of which the right to bear arms is fiercely emblematic.

Advocates frame their fight as a bulwark against tyranny, a safeguard of personal freedom and self-determination. They envision a world where self-reliance intersects with the prerogative of defense, a fundamental human condition sanctified by the founding fathers. Critics, on the other hand, call for a re-examination of priorities, emphasizing the need for public safety and the reduction of gun-related tragedies.

The media plays its own role, often portraying the conflict in stark binaries and fueling the fire with sensational reporting. Narratives are crafted in a way that feeds into the divisions rather than presenting a platform for nuanced dialogue and mutual understanding. This polarized landscape leaves little room for the middle ground, as individuals and groups entrench further into their ideological fortresses.

The industry around firearms, too, is deeply woven into this tapestry. It stands not only as a commercial entity but also as a symbol of resistance against what many perceive to be an encroaching government. The economic ramifications of gun legislation only heighten the stakes in a country where so many livelihoods are linked to the manufacture, sale, and ownership of guns.

Educational campaigns on both sides wage war over the minds of the populace, each asserting their interpretation of freedom and security. Gun rights advocates point to instances where firearms in the hands of the law-abiding have warded off aggression and saved lives, while control supporters highlight the potential for, and instances of, misuse and mass shootings.

Caught in the crossfire of this clash are the very citizens that the laws look to protect. Individuals navigate a labyrinth of conflicting information, trying to discern where their own views align within an embattled landscape. It becomes a personal journey as much as it is political, reflecting the very essence of what people believe about the role of government and the nature of liberty.

In the judiciary, courts interpret the boundaries of the Second Amendment with a gravity befitting the contentiousness of the subject. Legal battles ascend through the system, each verdict scrutinized for its fidelity to the Constitution or its perceived departure from the framers' intent. The Supreme Court, as the ultimate arbiter, weighs heavily on the trajectory of gun rights and restrictions in America.

What remains clear is that the culture war over guns is more than a simple policy debate—it's an examination of values and visions for the future of the nation. It represents the tension between collective security and individual rights, a balancing act of interests that is as delicate as it is profound.

As you stand at the crossroads of this pivotal issue, know that action is the sandstone upon which change is chiseled. Engagement in the political process is not only a right but an imperative for those who wish to help shape the narrative and outcome of this great debate. It calls for voices that are informed, passionate, and tempered with wisdom—a call to be part of something greater than oneself.

Remember, the war of ideologies is fought not only in legislatures and courtrooms but in the minds and hearts of citizens. It's a struggle that requires courage to confront complex issues, to engage in tough conversations, and to forge a path forward that best reflects the ideals enshrined in the Constitution.

Thus, the culture war over guns is emblematic of the broader struggle to maintain the integrity of Constitutional rights in the face of modern challenges. It is a vivid reminder that the preservation of liberty is a perpetual endeavor, demanding vigilance and participation from every corner of society.

In concluding this discourse, consider this: The culture war over guns, like any war, has its casualties and its victors. But ultimately, the greatest victory lies not in defeating the opposition, but in safeguarding the principles of the Constitution for future generations. In the pursuit of this goal, let individual conviction and collective action interlace to form the fabric of a nation that upholds its founding document with both reverence and relevance.

Chapter 5: Third and Fourth Amendments: Privacy and Property at Risk

In the shadow of the towering concerns surrounding the First and Second Amendments lies an equally crucial, yet often sidestepped discourse on our right to privacy and the sanctity of property—embodied in the Third and Fourth Amendments. These aren't just lines of text in an old document; they're the bedrock of our daily sense of security. Imagine your home, often seen as your ultimate sanctuary, morphing into a stage where others pull the strings without your consent. Here we unpack the stark realities of governmental overreach that creep into the very nooks and crannies of our personal lives. From the omnipresent surveillance apparatus that potentially ensnares our every move, to eminent domain policies that can wrestle away the ground beneath our feet, this shadow play of power infringes upon what we hold most dear. As we embark on this chapter, let's brace for an awakening—we're not just reclaiming paper rights; we're standing up for the soul of our personal liberty and the very essence of what it means to own a piece of the world.

The Forgotten Amendments Amid the ceaseless clamor over the more prominent amendments of the United States Constitution—the First, the Second, the Fifth, and so on—there lies a quiet, yet formidable set of regulations, often overlooked and underestimated in their significance. These are the Third and Fourth Amendments, core components of individual liberty, granting us protection from government intrusion into our homes and privacy. Yet, in today's digitalized and security-conscious world, these protections are under subtle siege, their implications far-reaching.

In this section, we explore these pivotal amendments—originally designed as a shield against the overreach of power and a guarantee of our civil liberties. Our focus remains on bringing these overshadowed elements of the Constitution into the light, revealing their current condition and urging a proactive response from every corner of the political spectrum. The understanding and defense of these rights are essential not only to our privacy and property but also to the foundational values of this Republic.

To begin, the Third Amendment, largely forgotten in the contemporary discourse, was born of a desire to maintain the sanctity of the individual's home. It prohibits the quartering of soldiers in private houses without the owner's consent, a stand against the abuses of the colonial era. Today, while the literal occupation of our homes by military forces is rare, the principle at stake still resonates—a fortress against the coercive presence of the state in our private lives. As citizens, it's crucial to discern modern parallels, ensuring our homes remain our sanctuaries.

The Fourth Amendment secures the right of the people to be free from unreasonable searches and seizures, underscoring the value of personal privacy. While this seems straightforward, the digital age presents complex challenges. Data mining, electronic surveillance, and other forms of digital intrusion pose fresh inquiries into what constitutes 'unreasonable' in a society where personal boundaries are blurred by technology. The principle enshrined in this amendment requires constant vigilance and interpretation to stay relevant in protecting us from unwarranted intrusions.

One might ask: how does this affect me directly? The answer lies in the subtle ways that invasive policies, sanctioned under the guise of public safety or efficiency, can erode private protections. Each GPS tracker, each security camera, each data collection algorithm represents a potential trespass into the domain that our forebears sought to guard. Awareness is the first defense; making informed choices regarding privacy is the second. Compliance through ignorance or apathy is the silent enemy.

Sidestepping these protections might seem justifiable in times of crisis or under the banner of combating crime or terrorism. However, history has shown that liberties once relinquished are seldom restored without a struggle. The trade-off between security and freedom is a false dichotomy; indeed, one can argue that there is no genuine security without foundational freedoms. Safeguarding these amendments is, therefore, not a question of prioritizing safety over privacy, but rather ensuring that both are preserved harmoniously.

Modern encroachments upon the Third and Fourth Amendments take many forms: from the use of eminent domain to repurpose private property without fair compensation to the mass collection of telephone metadata without individualized suspicion. Each instance, though perhaps seeming minor in isolation, compounds into a significant shift in the relationship between the state and the individual. Acknowledging these developments equips us to contend with them.

At the heart of it all is the concept of our home as a private refuge. When the government has the means to intrude upon our digital domiciles—our emails, our searches, our social media—without rigorous checks and balances, they challenge the very essence of these protections. Consent, historically a barrier to arbitrary authority, now requires a sophisticated understanding of the digital trespasses that are rarely made explicit to users.

The erosion of these rights does not occur in a vacuum. Each transgression against our liberties, in even the smallest degree, sets a precedent. These precedents, in their multiplicity, carve pathways that future policies can follow—often with more audacious intent. Recognizing this pattern provides the insight necessary to resist the gradual wearing down of our Constitutional safeguards.

In the task to hold the line, an active and informed citizenry is the most formidable instrument. It demands that we, as individuals and as a collective, comprehend and appreciate our own power to affect change. Engaging with the nuances of these "forgotten" amendments, navigating their modern implications, and challenging their dismissal or distortion is our right and responsibility.

The call to action is unequivocal. To maintain the liberties that define us as a free society, we must not let the overshadowing of critical amendments be our reality. Empowerment starts with knowledge—the knowledge of what is at stake and the knowledge of how to voice our dissent when faced with breaches of our constitutional protections.

Thus, let us rekindle our collective awareness and ensure that the Third and Fourth Amendments receive the recognition and respect they warrant. As pillars of our Constitution, they must not diminish into footnotes of history but should stand tall as emphatic affirmations of our inalienable rights. We must not be content with the narrative of forgotten amendments; we should be the authors of their revival.

Though we may not be barraged by headlines heralding the breaches of the Third or Fourth Amendments, the need for their stringent application is no less critical. Privacy and the sanctity of our homes and personal effects are quintessential American values that demand tireless champions. It is only through sustained engagement and the pursuit of accountability that these fundamental rights will endure.

Universally, our freedom is a reflection of our will to uphold the values enshrined in our founding documents. These amendments, once seen as self-evident expressions of our most basic rights, now call for a recognition renewed—a clarion call to action that insists on their unabated reverence and protection. Responding with informed intent can reshape the narrative that surrounds these foundational principles.

While the task may seem daunting, the rewards of preserving a free and fair society stand stark against the consequences of inertia. Each of us carries the potential to contribute to a legacy that treasures and safeguards the liberties we have inherited. It starts with valuing the foresight encapsulated within the "forgotten" amendments and extends to our unwavering commitment to defend their principles against all forms of encroachment.

As we chart a course forward, our clarity of purpose is as important as our resolve. The quest to uphold the forgotten amendments is indelibly linked to the broader endeavor to maintain a society that respects the rights of its members. It's the concerted efforts of informed individuals that can transform a nation, redirecting its governance towards true adherence to the Constitution—in spirit and letter. The forgotten amendments need not remain so; they can be remembered, revered, and fully realized in our era. It is up to us to ensure that this becomes our shared reality.

Surveillance State: Encroachment on Privacy

In a landscape where liberty once stood unchallenged, a chilling breeze has begun to swirl, whispering of change, of a horizon obscured by the darkening shadow of surveillance. This awareness isn't refined to the realms of fiction or the paranoid rants of a conspiratorial minority. It is real, verifiable, and steadily expanding, puncturing the trust between citizen and state. It is the emergence of a surveillance state—an architecture meticulously crafted to monitor and record the daily interactions of its citizens without their consent.

The Fourth Amendment, designed as the bulwark of privacy, guarantees protection against unreasonable searches and seizures. Yet, since the advent of the digital age and the fallout from harrowing events of terror, the spheres of privacy envisioned by the founding fathers are contracting at an alarming pace. Surveillance technologies have burgeoned and so has their appetite for data—your data. Through this lens, the Constitution appears not as the living document it's purported to be, but more a historical artifact, failing to shield the citizenry from the prying eyes of omnipresent surveillance.

Tread carefully does the government when it cloaks its acts in the guise of security. Yet, one can't help but question: at what cost to freedom? The thin line between security and liberty becomes blurred as databases swell with our personal details, phone calls, internet searches, and even the rhythms of our daily lives, all collated, cross-referenced, and stored for purposes opaque to the public eye.

The scope of this surveillance doesn't end with data collection. It extends into the very heart of our democratic processes. Dissent, once the proud hallmark of democracy, is now often seen through the skeptical lens of state security, with activists and critics finding themselves targets of investigation. The state's justification? A nebulous definition of 'national safety'—one which becomes, ever so conveniently, what the authorities need it to be at any given time.

Consider the potency of surveillance utilizing the vast capabilities of modern technology. Drones, once far-off emblems of warfare, skulk domestic skies, capturing footage from angles the human eye cannot reach. Our smartphones, lauded for their convenience, double as tracking devices, logging every movement, even in the quiet of night. Social media platforms, those digital town squares for public discourse, have morphed into data mines, their algorithms dissecting our preferences, inclinations, and affiliations.

It is an unspoken exchange—bits of privacy chipped away for the promise of safety. However, this promise is tenuous at best. Security without scrutiny breeds an environment ripe for abuse. Once equipped with such tools of surveillance, it becomes temptingly easy for the state to extend its reach, to justify the unjustifiable under the shroud of 'combatting threats.'

But one must ponder the nature of these 'threats.' When a child's backpack is RFID-tagged for attendance tracking, when social credit systems judge worthiness for travel or services, when biometric data from innocent individuals is stored indefinitely—what threat are we countering? Or have we rather become the unwitting participants in a grand experiment, forfeiting inch by inch the fundamental rights we once believed untouchable?

The question is not whether surveillance technologies should exist. The digital world brings complexities that necessitate some form of oversight. The critical question is this: how do we maintain a balance where surveillance tools are not wielded to erode the core values of personal autonomy and freedom? Vigilance must be our watchword, legal restraints our shield, transparency our guiding light, and accountability our relentless cry.

Amidst this unraveling tapestry of privacy, realize the potency you hold as an individual—your power to question, to challenge, to demand reform. Let us not be passive onlookers in the construction of the very chains that seek to bind us. We must ignite conversations, push for policy changes, and engage in continual litigation to test the elasticity of our rights. The tide of public opinion can turn the course of legislative action, solidifying our cries against unwarranted intrusion into a resounding chorus, seeking to reclaim the ground we stand on.

Shed light on the subject, shed complacency, and take a firm stance. The guardianship of privacy should not be a reactionary measure, provoked only by the overstep of authority. It must be proactive, woven into the normative fabric of our societal values. Empowerment begins with understanding. Know the laws, challenge their application, demand strict oversight, and never accept at face value the narrative that for the cost of your privacy comes the reward of security.

Privacy in its purest form is the sacred right to create, express, and live without the heavy-handed intervention of the state. It's the right to be let alone—the grand rehearsal space for the individual to explore and define who they are, separate from societal pressures and, certainly, separate from governmental voyeurism. In the end, privacy is the cornerstone upon which the integrity of the individual is erected, and it must be fiercely protected.

In the annals of history, it has always been the vigilant who steer the direction of change, who refuse to accept the dissolution of rights as a necessary evil. The surveillance state may be encroaching, but the strength of an informed, spirited citizenry remains the best defense against this encroachment. Take up the mantle of this defense—engage in the civic duty to uphold the liberties enshrined in the Constitution, for a future that reveres privacy as the birthright of every individual.

It would be all too simple to resign ourselves to this reality as the new normal. Yet, we must resist. We must dissect and challenge the policies that allow these practices. We must hold our elected officials to account, for they are stewards of our liberties. With fortitude and relentless dedication to the cause of freedom, we can dismantle the apparatus of the surveillance state and restore the privacy once promised by the Constitution. The pursuit is neither simple nor without sacrifice, but it is necessary for the mantle of liberty to remain untarnished for generations to come.

Remember, history does not just narrate the actions of the mighty. It also recalls the resistance of the steadfast. Your voice is potent. Your action, imperative. Together, the concept of Big Brother can be confined to the pages of fiction, where it belongs. Rise, engage, and demand a future where privacy is not a privilege to be eroded but a right to be cherished and protected.

Eminent Domain and the Battle for Property
introduces a pivotal conflict in the landscape of American
rights. Imagine a home passed down through generations,
a family business built from scratch, or a farm tended by
the same hands that sowed its first seeds. In each mosaic
of memories, we see the flesh and blood of the American
dream—ownership and heritage. But what happens when
the government, brandishing the sword of eminent
domain, lays claim to what citizens hold dear? This is
where our vigilance must be as unbending as the steel of
that sword.

The power of eminent domain allows the government to
seize private property for public use, crediting 'just
compensation' to those displaced. This tool, inscribed
within the Takings Clause of the Fifth Amendment, is a
double-edged blade—champion of progress and fiend to
the proprietor. Integral projects like roads, schools, and
hospitals can necessitate such takings, but where is the
line drawn, and who ensures it isn't crossed?

History hums with the tales of this strife. Cases like Kelo
vs. City of New London recalibrated the understanding of
'public use', widening it to include economic
development, a decision that roused the ire of many. This
ruling illuminated the often murky waters of eminent
domain, throwing into sharp relief the question: Was this
a perversion of a constitutional safeguard?

As citizens, understanding our rights is akin to a sentinel
knowing their post. It serves not only as a shield but as a
sword against encroachments. Arm yourself with
knowledge; what is public use, what constitutes just
compensation, and when does your government overstep
its bounds?

In the arena of eminent domain, the process itself can be as punishing as the outcome. The notification, the hearings, the valuations—each step can be a goliath to a David without sling or stone. When the government exercises this power, it wields more than just the law—it commands a cortege of resources: lawyers, analysts, and consultants.

You must not be passive in this battle. Scrutinize the negotiated price; it often fails to reflect the true losses. Consider the cases where 'just compensation' discounts the emotional lineage woven into the property's fabric. Courts can side with homeowners challenging inadequate valuations, but these David v. Goliath victories are hard-won and rarer than we're led to believe.

The power dynamics at play poke at the very heart of ownership. If your domain is not definitively your own, if it hangs by the thread of governmental need—how can we say we truly own anything at all? Our forefathers erected our rights to prevent the might of many from crushing the will of one; property rights are no less sacrosanct.

Imagine the futures forged in the fires of these confrontations—futures where the spheres of governmental reach and individual rights are clearly defined. A keystone in this architecture is precedent, legal bedrock on which future rulings are made. With each battle, with every ruling, this foundation is either fortified or eroded. Citizens' actions—or their silence—shape these outcomes.

Mobilize beyond the theoretical. Learn and engage with the processes that govern eminent domain. It's not uncommon to find local governments stretching the bounds of 'public benefit' to seize land for financially lucrative private developments. The bulwark against such transgressions is an informed, proactive citizenry, ever-ready to hold their representatives accountable.

Organize, advocate, and educate others about the power and peril of eminent domain. As the fabric of property rights is stretched, it is common people—bonded by a shared vision of fairness and justice—who can mend the tears. Broad public outrage and legislative reform often walk hand-in-hand, as seen in the aftermath of controversial rulings.

Your land, your home, your business—it's not merely an asset, it's a fortress of individual liberty. Eminent domain, when employed judiciously, serves the greater good. Yet when misused, it transforms from government tool to tyrant's weapon. In the balance of these extremes, justice must be the weight that tips the scales.

Perceive the battles of our time; private homes razed for commercial plazas, family farms seized for industrial expansion, ancestral homesteads claimed for pipelines. Is this the 'public use' our constitutional architects envisioned? Or is this the manifestation of a modern Leviathan, stretching beyond the intended reach of our founding blueprint?

Foster resilience, for the fight is not solely out in field or court. It is also in the blissful quiet of your own backyard, where the specter of eminent domain looms unseen until the day it knocks at your door. Insist on transparency, demand adherence to the spirit of the law, and, when necessary, challenge its application in the halls of justice.

The battle for property is not won by might alone but by the relentless spirit of the guard. Align that spirit with a jurisdictional shield—an understanding of your rights and a readiness to assert them. Stand poised in defense of your property, for the home you save may one day be your own.

Ultimately, in the clash between private ownership and public purpose, we must not cede ground to apathy or resignation. Remember that the flame of liberty is kept alive by those who nurture its light and stand watch against the encroaching darkness. Eminent domain, a necessary power in the hands of government, must always be guided by a compass of fairness and constancy. Our vigilance as citizens ensures the path it follows remains just.

Chapter 6: Fifth Amendment: Protecting the Accused

The very parchment of the Constitution radiates with the intent to protect the individual from the might of the state, and at the helm of this philosophy sits the Fifth Amendment, a cornerstone in the architecture of justice. This chapter peels back the layers of due process, a principle under siege in a world where immediacy trumps investigation, where the watermark of guilt is often pressed upon the accused before a full hearing. Through an unwavering lens, we'll scrutinize the dance between confessions and the coercion that choreographs them, all too often behind the justice system's curtain. Furthermore, we cannot ignore the controversial practice of asset forfeiture and the chilling mantra it sings: guilty until proven innocent. In a system that should presume innocence, it's crucial to remain vigilant—to understand that these rights, set as safeguards, are more than legal jargon; they're the fiber that binds the fabric of our freedoms. Let's navigate this with a critical spirit, acknowledging that once lost, such protections are not easily reclaimed, and that erosion of these rights is erosion of our collective liberty.

Due Process in Jeopardy The cornerstone of criminal justice in the United States, the principle of due process, is enshrined in the Fifth Amendment of the Constitution. It dictates that the state must respect all legal rights owed to a person. This section scrutinizes the current health of due process in America, lifting the veil on situations where these fundamental protections are not just at risk but are being actively undermined.

Imagine you're walking down the street, you're suddenly arrested, not told why, and held indefinitely without charge. This scenario may seem far-fetched, yet variations of it play out more frequently than one might expect. There is a troubling pattern emerging where the rights to a fair hearing and trial are becoming casualties in the name of expediency or national security.

The erosion can be subtle. It starts with small exceptions, a waiver here or there, justified under extraordinary circumstances. Yet, those exceptions start carving into the bedrock of due process, creating pathways for abuse. Little by little, the assurance that justice will be blind, fair, and impartial becomes less certain.

Think of the accused who sits in jail for months, sometimes years before trial because of bureaucratic backlogs. Or those who are pressured into plea bargains because they are told the system is too overloaded to afford them a trial. This isn't just an infringement on their rights; it's a systemic failure that chips away at the integrity of due process.

The concept of innocent until proven guilty seems to be wavering. Asset forfeiture, a controversial law enforcement tool, allows seizure of property suspected of involvement in crime, without necessarily charging the owner with wrongdoing. Stories of individuals fighting to get back their property—often without the means to challenge the government in court—point to due process being more theory than practice.

Consider also those individuals stuck in a Kafkaesque limbo under the banner of national security. They're held without trial, sometimes for years, in military or immigration detention centers. Here, due process isn't just jeopardized; it seems entirely discarded, an inconvenient obstacle to certain agendas.

Electronic surveillance has ushered in a new frontier in due process challenges. One's right to private communication and protection from unreasonable searches is impinged upon as government agencies harvest data on a grand scale. In places unseen and unacknowledged, personal information is screened and scrutinized without one's knowledge or consent, let alone a warrant.

The fusion of powerful technology with government reach has outpaced the checks and balances intended to protect citizens. When the digital footprint you leave behind every day becomes fodder for surveillance without oversight, it's not just privacy that's lost; due process is side-stepped in the process.

Vigilance is necessary when laws, initially passed with the noble intent to protect, are repurposed in ways that test the boundaries of constitutionality. The Patriot Act is one such piece of legislation whose broad scope has sparked critical debate around due process rights. Its impact continues to resonate, raising questions about the balance between security and civil liberties.

Even beyond national borders, the extrajudicial reach of drone strikes calls into question the value placed on due process. When decisions of life and death are made based on metadata, we stray far from the constitutional guarantees that require judgment to be passed by one's peers and in accordance with the law.

But here's the crux: due process is not just a legal technicality; it's the manifest expression of humanity in the justice system. To chip away at due process is to chip away at the moral compass of the nation. It's a journey down a path where the ends justify the means, yet history repeatedly shows the peril of such a trajectory.

There is power in awareness and in the collective outcry for justice. Each time a person stands up for due process, they stand up not only for themselves but for every citizen. It's a message that impunity has no place in a society that prizes fairness, and that the Constitution isn't a mere recommendation, but a binding promise of equitable treatment under the law.

The pushback against the decline of due process can't be left to a few. It's a responsibility that lies with all who believe in the principles laid down by the founders of the nation. It's time to confront these challenges, not through violence or vitriol, but through the very systems that embody our democratic ideals, to ensure they work for all, not just a select few.

Due process may be in jeopardy, but it's not beyond salvation. It remains one of the most profound principles that can be wielded by the judiciary to curb the excesses of the other branches of government. While the currents pushing against it are strong, the dedication to justice and fairness must be stronger.

Empowerment begins with understanding and the willingness to challenge status quo complacency. Each individual must become an advocate for due process, engaging in civic discourse, educating themselves and others, and holding those in power accountable. The story of due process in America is still being written, and it's up to its citizens to ensure it's a story of triumph and not tragedy.

Confessions and Coercion in the Justice System

Moving deeper into the terrain of the Fifth Amendment, an issue stands starkly before us. A cornerstone of fairness in the justice system—confessions must be voluntary to be admissible in the court of law. But what happens when coercion taints this process? When individuals, caught in the intimidating maze of interrogation, find themselves confessing to crimes they didn't commit? This is a reality in too many cases, and the cost is nothing less than the very essence of justice. The landscape is sometimes grim, and the practice of coercion creates a chasm between the ideal and the real.

Coercion is not merely a physical act; the psychological strain during interrogations can lead individuals to break under pressure. The tools of the coercer are manifold – from sleep deprivation to the relentless hammering of accusations, the balance scales of justice tip wildly under such fraught circumstances. The stakes? The very liberty, the very life, of the accused, funneled down the dark path of miscarried justice.

Understand this; the integrity of a confession is paramount. It's the solid ground on which so much of a prosecution may rest. But when that ground is quaking— shaken by tactics that would make the innocent speak just to end their torment—where does that leave faith in the system? To acknowledge this breach is not to undermine the work of the dedicated individuals in law enforcement but to call forth a commitment to truth that supersedes the fleeting satisfaction of a solved case.

It's essential to confront the uncomfortable truth that false confessions are not outliers; they are proven occurrences, highlighted in overturned convictions where DNA evidence has shattered previous certainties. It's not about whether coercion happens; it's about acknowledging its presence and taking determined steps to prevent it. It's about protecting not just the right to a fair trial but the road leading up to it.

Let's talk about safeguards. Mirandize rights are one such protection, designed to arm the citizens with the knowledge of their right to silence and legal counsel. Yet, the effectiveness of these rights hangs precariously on the assumption that all individuals can comprehend and assert them against a tide of authority. We must consider how factors such as age, mental ability, and the stress of the situation might dilute these protections.

Data speaks volumes and the tales spun by the numbers are telling. Innocent Project statistics illuminate a stark reality where false confessions are present in a significant portion of wrongful convictions. This is not a problem confined to the fringes; it reaches into the core of the justice system.

The pursuit of truth must be unwavering, yet it should not sacrifice the principles on which the justice system stands. Interrogation practices exist that are both effective and ethical. The introduction of such practices on a wider scale stands as a testament that coercion need not be the companion of confession.

Recognition of the problem plays a critical role. Training law enforcement to differentiate between coercion and legitimate interrogation techniques is essential. Likewise, recording interrogations in their entirety provides a level of transparency that serves both the accused and the integrity of the justice system.

Consider for a moment the weight of being accused, the gravitational pull of the authoritative voice across the table telling you that the evidence points to one undeniable conclusion: your guilt. Now imagine, within this gravity, not guilt, but innocence. The burden is crushing, and suspicion becomes a beast too great to bear alone. This is where legal representation becomes not just a right but a lifeline.

Legal counsel must be readily accessible, regardless of wealth or status. In an arena where words can seal fate, the right to an attorney stands as a column of justice. Public defenders work tirelessly, but the system can overwhelm with scale and pace, at times leaving the indigent defendant with less than the ardent defense required.

The constitutional promise of the Fifth Amendment—to be free from self-incrimination—hangs in balance. It's an assurance that is neither negotiable nor expendable. To support and uphold this promise is to affirm a commitment to due process and to reflect the values inscribed in the Constitution itself. It's about reinforcing the foundation, not merely reshaping the surface. To assign blame without ample reflection or rectification does not serve progress. Rather, it's insight followed by action that leads to reform.

Concrete steps like improving the quality of public defense and enforcing strict adherence to ethical interrogation standards are answers to the call of the Constitution. They are statements that declare, unequivocally, that the justice system values accuracy over assumption and dignity over disgrace.

Encouraging oversight by independent bodies to review cases of alleged coercion can serve to provide checks and balances within the justice system. This could result in the establishment of review commissions, which bring together legal experts, policymakers, and citizens, to ensure that justice is not merely a concept, but a living, breathing ideal in every case.

The narrative of coercion and confession in the justice system is at a critical juncture. The conversation is not about coddling the guilty but about ensuring that the right person is held accountable. It's about standing not against authority, but for fairness; not for doubt, but for certainty; not for haste, but for due process. And most certainly, it is about defending and upholding a Constitution that allows the nation to call itself a realm of justice and fairness.

By recognizing, resisting, and reforming any practices that contaminate the pure pursuit of truth, citizens themselves become the guardians of their rights. The power of the Constitution is not merely in its words, but in the vigilant eyes that watch over it and the fearless voices that speak out to defend it. This is the promise of the Fifth Amendment, the armor against coercion, and the heart of a just society.

Asset Forfeiture: Guilty Until Proven Innocent?

Imagine for a moment a system where your possessions can be confiscated by the state without the formality of a criminal charge, let alone a conviction. Does that sound like a plot borrowed from a dystopian novel? The reality is more immediate, and it unfolds under the auspices of asset forfeiture laws. These laws, often defended as tools in the war on drugs and organized crime, equip federal and state law enforcement agencies with the power to seize property suspected of being connected to criminal activity.

Now, the concept of punishing the wheelings and dealings of high-flying crime syndicates has a cathartic ring to it. No argument there. But when the dragnet indiscriminately captures everyday citizens, it's an entirely different narrative—one where innocent until proven guilty blurs into its very antithesis.

Deep at the heart of the Fifth Amendment lies the guarantee that no person shall be deprived of life, liberty, or property without due process of law. However, asset forfeiture often skirts the boundary of due process, operating in a landscape where property rights are not as steadfast as one may assume.

Under civil asset forfeiture, law enforcement can seize assets like money, cars, and real estate without filing charges against the property owner. Let that sink in for a moment. It's not necessarily about what you did; it's about what your property was allegedly involved in. Under such a premise, could your hard-earned assets be at risk? Absolutely, if there's a suspicion they were involved in a crime, no matter how tenuous the link.

But how could such a paradox exist under the Constitution's vigilant eye? The rationale behind civil asset forfeiture pivots on a legal curiosity wherein the property itself is charged with involvement in a crime, not the owner. Thus, to recover the seized assets, the owner must prove the property's innocence—a Kafkaesque twist that turns the fundamental principle of justice on its head.

While drug barons and criminal overlords should definitely be divested of their ill-gotten gains, the reach of asset forfeiture has extended to ensnare those far from the criminal mastermind archetype. Simple misunderstandings or proximity to unrelated illegal activity can result in the financial ruin of individuals who find themselves in the wrong place at the wrong time.

Stories abound of law enforcement seizing cash savings from individuals during routine traffic stops with claims that it's drug money, simply because the amount appears suspicious. Others have lost homes because a relative, unbeknownst to them, committed a crime on the premises. The burden of proof shifts from the state to the citizen—a dynamic riddled with potential for abuse and a clear departure from the presumption of innocence.

To challenge asset forfeiture, one must navigate a legal labyrinth potentially more costly than the property's value. The adversarial process can overwhelm those without vast resources. The conundrum they face results in many forgoing the fight altogether—an outcome that stands as a testament to an imbalanced justice system.

Supporters of asset forfeiture highlight its effectiveness as a law enforcement tool that disrupts criminal enterprises by draining their resources. They contend that it curbs illegal activities by hitting where it hurts: the pocketbook. However, it becomes inherently problematic when the pursuit of justice morphs into an enterprise generating revenue for law enforcement at the expense of civil liberties. Transparency around the use and distribution of forfeited assets is not always adequately maintained, leading to questions about the incentives at play.

Fundamentally, the practice pits the might of government against the rights of individuals. It serves as a poignant reminder that remaining vigilant about our constitutional rights is not only prudent but necessary. The safeguards of liberty and property are neither self-executing nor unassailable; they demand constant scrutiny and unfettered advocacy.

Mobilizing to demand reform and accountability in the use of asset forfeiture is more than a rallying cry—it's a bulwark against the erosion of fundamental freedoms. Engaged citizenship must go beyond mere awareness to encompass calls to action, driving home the message to our legislators and enforcers: constitutional boundaries must be respected.

Revisiting the tenets and processes underpinning asset forfeiture is not just about restoring trust in the justice system; it's about upholding values that form the bedrock of a free society. When property can be convicted without a trial and owners must prove innocence rather than the state proving guilt, we're looking at a troubling inversion of justice. An inversion that has no place in a constitutional republic where the rule of law is paramount.

Asset forfeiture reform calls for a recalibration of the scales of justice, where due process rights are as robust as the protections against theft and where innocent individuals do not bear the burden of a legal system gone awry. This is not just about rebalancing legal power—it's about holding steadfast to the moral compass that guides our national conscience.

We must rise with unwavering determination to protect what is rightfully ours, ensuring that the age-old maxim of innocence until proven guilty remains untarnished. And in doing so, we honor the wisdom of those who framed the delicate architecture of our Constitution, trusting that it is our collective resolve that will sustain justice for all within a land that prides itself on the principles of freedom and fairness.

Chapter 7: Sixth Amendment: The Fading Right to a Fair Trial

Embedded in the heart of American justice, the Sixth Amendment was a beacon of hope, insisting on fairness within the scales of justice, yet its gleam dims under modern-day scrutiny. Vigilance is essential, as without it, rights to a speedy and public trial, once held as sacrosanct, drift into the recesses of obscurity, overtaken by judicial delays and closed-door proceedings. Consider the erosion of a cornerstone: the right to a trial by an impartial jury—a sacred tenet in our legal ethos, now vanishing behind plea bargains and settlements. This chapter waves a flag, not of surrender, but of rallying intent. To reclaim the essence of the Sixth Amendment, citizens must awaken to its wane. The fight for justice is not a spectator sport—it's an arena where endurance and resolve must prevail. The fading of fundamental rights isn't simply a footnote in a legal textbook, but a slow bleed of the liberties which, if left unaddressed, mark the undoing of fair trial promises made over two centuries past.

Speedy Trial or Judicial Delay? Justice moves with a deliberate pace in a society governed by law. Yet, when justice stirs too slowly, the scales tip unfavorably against the very foundation of liberty. The Sixth Amendment guarantees the right to a swift and fair trial. It's time to grapple with the bitter truth: countless individuals languish in a legal limbo for months, even years, awaiting their day in court. This isn't just an inconvenience; it's a critical lapse in the system promised to us.

The tragically ironic part of this situation is that speed is not just a courtesy—it's a constitutional imperative. Forget a mere goal; a speedy trial is a right that lies at the heart of a functioning democracy. It protects the innocent from protracted periods of uncertainty and the indignity of prolonged detention. It's a safeguard against the loss of critical evidence, fading memories, and by extension, justice itself.

Why the delays? The courts, inundated with cases, face backlogs of monumental proportions. The shortages of public defenders add to this morass, placing a strain on the ability to mount timely defenses. It can seem less like an orderly queue and more like a dam on the verge of bursting.

When the judicial system dawdles, the ripple effects are profound. Individuals may lose their jobs, homes, and custody of their children solely because their case is stuck in limbo. Families are dismantled, and lives are put on hold. Stress compounds; despair festers.

Consider the impact on society. Confidence in legal institutions wanes as justice appears elusive for the common person. The right to a speedy trial isn't a luxury—when eroded, it sends tremors through communities, challenging their belief in the very essence of a fair and democratic society.

Actions speak louder than words, and in the halls of justice, the cacophony of inaction is deafening. Any talk of honoring constitutional rights feels hollow when juxtaposed with the lived reality of countless individuals awaiting their so-called swift justice. Enough talk. It's high time for a judicious blend of resolve and ingenuity to steer the course.

Technology presents a beacon of hope. Virtual courts, online filings, and electronic monitoring can slash delays. Yet adoption is slow, mired in a mélange of bureaucracy and hesitation. Innovation requires a daring leap, not a timid step.

Furthermore, this isn't merely about logistics—it's about aligning principles with practice. What's needed is a courageous recalibration of the judicial process. It demands political will, legal finesse, and public support. It requires championing an unwavering commitment to the Constitution's spirit by ensuring that its promises hold true in practice, not just in parchment.

The disturbing reality of unnecessary incarceration before trial is more than a legal issue—it's a potent symbol of a system failing to uphold its own ideals. The idea that one is innocent until proven guilty seems a distant echo when handcuffed by time.

Is the Sixth Amendment's guarantee of a speedy trial an endangered principle? Perhaps it is, but it's not extinct. There remains a path lit by determination and a deep-seated belief in the primacy of what that right stands for. It's a call to action for a systemic makeover—a rallying cry for a rebirth of justice served without delay.

Reform is not just a possibility; it is an urgent necessity. We must streamline procedures, invest in resources, and prioritize the swift resolution of cases to uphold the integrity of the legal process. This isn't a job for the hesitant; it requires men and women who can push against the inertia of tradition.

To those ensnared by the slow turn of the judicial wheel, know this: your plight is not unseen. Every delayed trial is a blemish on the collective conscience of a nation that asserts itself as the land of the free. It's not just your fight; it's ours as a society that values justice.

Imagine a system where time in court is determined by the merits of the case, not by the sluggishness of the docket. Envision a judicial process where every second counts—not just the final judgment. That's the promise of the Sixth Amendment. It's a promise overdue, yet one that we must strive, relentlessly, to fulfill.

So, where do you stand—in the shadow of delay or in the light of prompt justice? Your voice matters. Engage with the issue, demand reform, support improvements. The question of a speedy trial or judicial delay rests in the hands of the informed and the engaged.

As we continue this exploration into constitutional rights, let us carry forward the charge to preserve and protect the Sixth Amendment. The challenge is monumental, but the stakes are nothing less than our liberty and our faith in justice. This isn't just a chapter in a book; it's a pivotal moment in our history. As citizens of this republic, the power to drive change towards a just, fair, and efficient legal system is in our hands. Together, let's ensure the right to a speedy trial is not just a constitutional pledge, but a living, breathing reality for all.

Public Trial or Secret Proceedings? Think about the concept of a fair trial—not as an abstract term, but as a tangible, vital pillar upholding the freedom of every individual facing judgement by their government. The Sixth Amendment carves out this principle, binding it to the very soul of American jurisprudence. Yet, a question hangs heavy like a cloud above our heads: do we, as a society, still uphold the sanctity of a public trial, or have we slid down the slippery slope towards secret proceedings?

In recent times, there is a trend where the balance seems to teeter perilously. Cases once considered clear-cut for public purview are occasionally shrouded in veils of secrecy. These secret proceedings threaten to undermine the bedrock of democracy. In the name of national security or the protection of sensitive information, courtrooms—symbolic of transparency and justice—are now sometimes closing their doors to the public eye.

Why does this matter? One may ponder the significance, especially in an age where the efficiency of closed-door operations entices the time-strapped masses. Public trials serve as a check on judicial abuses, keep prosecutorial misconduct in line, and ensure that judges and attorneys adhere to the highest ethical standards. Remove the public from the equation, and the courtroom becomes a place where the scales of justice can be tipped undetected.

Closed proceedings wave a red flag. They raise unsettling questions—what is being hidden, and why? In the absence of accountability, darkness encroaches upon the light, and the rights of defendants can be eclipsed. The precedence of secret trials gradually erodes trust, as citizens grow suspect of what their government does behind closed doors. The alarm bells ring clear; this trajectory imperils the very essence of public confidence.

Awareness is the first step. Knowledge of the shift from public to secretive litigation must seep into the collective consciousness. Each citizen should understand the implications these covert actions carry for personal freedom and societal structure. Without the vigilant eye of the public, power can, and often does, go unchecked.

Fight for justice to be visible. Advocate for transparency, not just for those who stand accused, but for everyone. For each secret proceeding accepted, a thread is pulled from the fabric of constitutional rights—perhaps subtly unnoticed at first, but potentially unraveling the whole over time. This issue does not simply affect the current climate; it forecasts a shadow over future legal landscapes and civic awareness.

Demand the light, not just for yourself, but for generations to come. When trials occur in the shadows, the truth becomes elusive, and liberty pays the price. Conscious of the creeping threat, it is our duty to staunchly defend the Sixth Amendment's guarantee of a public trial, recognizing this not as a privilege, but as an inalienable right essential to preserving justice.

Consider the journeys of other nations down paths veiled in secrecy. Draw from their stories lessons and warnings. Place those learnings like stones on the path to prevent sliding towards a future where secret courts are the norm rather than the chilling exception. Understand that secrecy feeds not upon reason but fear, and once allowed to take hold, it seldom loosens its grip.

Challenge the status quo boldly. Invoke the constitutional commitment to openness in proceedings where the public's exclusion is sought. Stand firm in the belief that the arc of moral justice bends towards transparency and that secreting away the processes of justice is contrary to that end. The more voices rise in unison, the more authorities must listen, and the stronger the fabric of liberty becomes.

Mobilize intellect and intent towards upholding a free and open judicial system. Engage in discourse, hold dialogues with representatives, and become the embodiment of the oversight that a public trial is meant to ensure. Never underestimate the power of collective will in forging change. For in this engagement lies the true meaning of a government by the people and for the people.

Guard vigilantly against the encroaching shadows. Every secret court docket, every undisclosed hearing, is a signpost on the road away from freedom. It is in the interest of freedom that secrecy must be the exception, not the rule—applied with the utmost caution and under the scrutiny of rigorous justifications.

In achieving balance, calibrate the scales. Recognize that there are cases where some measure of secrecy is needed to protect identities, sensitive evidence, or national security. However, blanket acceptance of secrecy cannot prevail. Mark the distinction with precision; discretion should be applied sparingly and always under the consideration that a departure from public scrutiny is a serious deviation from constitutional norms.

Refuse to surrender rights in silence. Demand that closed proceedings be justified publicly and that the reasons withstand the strictest scrutiny. As citizens, it is vital to remember that the judiciary is not above the people it serves and must be held accountable within the framework of our Constitution and legal system.

Be the sentinel for justice. Uphold the Sixth Amendment, not just as an observer but as an active participant in the pursuit of a transparent and fair judicial process. When secret proceedings threaten to become a commonplace, when the light of public trial dims, it is upon the shoulders of vigilant citizens to cast that light anew.

Thus, the eternal question persists: Public trial or secret proceedings? The answer must affirm the immutable value of transparency and the unwavering dedication to a constitutional promise. In this fight for openness, engage with courage, drawn from the wellspring of rights and responsibilities that the Constitution provides. Let the quest for justice, held squarely in the public's gaze, be the legacy that defines a generation steadfast in the preservation of liberty.

The Vanishing Trial By Jury The Sixth Amendment of the United States Constitution secures the right to a trial by an impartial jury, a cornerstone of American justice since its inception. Yet, in today's courtrooms, the very fabric of this right is fraying, imperceptibly to many, yet alarmingly clear upon closer inspection. In this critical exploration, let's illuminate how and why the trial by jury is vanishing, the ramifications for citizens and society, and why it matters to uphold this pivotal right.

Historically, a trial by jury has served as a bulwark against potential government overreach, ensuring that peers—ordinary citizens—have the final say in the most severe legal disputes. It is a profoundly democratic practice, predicated on the belief that collective wisdom and the collective conscience provide the fairest shot at justice.

Consider the changes in our judicial landscape. Alarmingly, statistics reveal a sharp decline in the percentage of legal disputes being resolved by juries. Plea bargains, dismissals, and summary judgments are replacing jury trials at an unprecedented rate. This shift might seem practical on the surface—an efficient way to handle an ever-growing caseload. However, the implications for justice and individual rights are profound and disturbing.

Why the shift away from jury trials? Several factors conspire to steer cases out of the courtroom. Mandatory minimum sentencing laws, for instance, have given prosecutors excessive leverage, often coercing defendants into plea bargains out of fear of facing the full force of these predetermined sentences.

The cost of litigation serves as another formidable barrier. Engaging in a courtroom battle can bankrupt individuals or small businesses, leaving them no choice but to settle disputes outside of court. Furthermore, the complexity of the legal system can intimidate those without resources, pushing them toward alternatives that may not serve their interests or the cause of justice.

Jury trials have become so rare that many refer to it as "legal extinction." The decline is not just about the numbers; it signals a drift away from citizen participation in the justice system, a foundational concept of the republic. In its absence, the gap between the law and public sentiment widens, breeding distrust and apathy toward the judicial process.

The fallout of this erosion is not just conceptual; it has tangible effects on civil liberties. When jury trials vanish, so does the chance for a defendant to have their case heard in full, for the evidence to be thoroughly examined, and for justice to be publicly scrutinized and served. The systemic pressure to avoid a "risky" jury trial marginalizes the truth-seeking purpose of the justice system, undermining both accountability and transparency.

Jury service also has an educative function. It instills a sense of civic duty, provides firsthand experience with the judicial process, and secures a democratic check on the laws applied in courts. As this experience becomes rarer, public understanding of and respect for the justice system can diminish. This distancing effect weakens the societal fabric, as governance seems to shift from the public realm into the hands of a legal elite.

Think of the stories not told and the precedents not set when jury trials decline. The narrative of justice that unfolds in an open courtroom reflects the values and principles of a society. With fewer jury trials, the societal dialogue about what justice means is stunted, and the law may grow distant from the people it's intended to serve.

In addressing this quandary, imperative questions arise: How can the balance be restored? How do we safeguard the promise of a trial by jury without compromising the efficiency a modern justice system requires? The challenge is to reconcile these seemingly competing interests without sacrificing the principles of fairness, accountability, and transparency that underlie the right to a trial by jury.

One potential solution lies in reforming the very mechanisms that push cases away from jury trials. Adjusting mandatory minimum laws, reassessing plea bargain practices, and making litigation costs less daunting could encourage more defendants to exercise their Sixth Amendment rights.

Further, technology offers new avenues for efficiency in the legal system. Virtual hearings and other technological innovations, while not replacements for actual jury trials, can lessen the logistical hurdles that contribute to the decline in their numbers.

When individuals understand the gravity of their role as jurors, the right becomes easier to protect. Therefore, public education about this right and the broader civic duty associated with it is essential. A public that values and understands the jury's purpose is a public more likely to fight for its preservation.

The vanishing trial by jury is symptomatic of a justice system in flux, caught between the tenets of traditional jurisprudence and the pressures of modern governance. How we address this shift will define the integrity of our justice system. Remember, once lost, a right is exceedingly difficult to resurrect. If we are to protect ourselves from unjust persecution, the time to act is now, safeguarding this essential right to a trial by our peers. Couple this with fervent advocacy and intentional legal reform, and the trial by jury can be fortified for future generations.

As we transition into the examination of civil litigation under fire, we carry with us the weight of this vanishing right. Civil trials by jury are also under threat, and the initiatives we discuss next will further illustrate the necessity of our shared vigilance. Remember, it is not the walls of a courtroom that uphold justice; it is the unwavering commitment of its citizens to the democratic principles upon which it was founded.

Chapter 8: Seventh and Eighth Amendments: Civil Trials and Cruel Punishments

Emerging from the shadows of previous chapters, we pivot to a critical junction in our constitutional understanding: the Seventh and Eighth Amendments. These amendments safeguard our rights in civil trials and protect against excessive or inhumane punishment. They're not just lines of text from a bygone era; they're living, breathing testaments to fairness and humanity. However, these vital protections are facing relentless pressure. The integrity of civil litigation teeters on a precarious edge as individuals question the efficacy of a jury of peers amid a landscape marred by expensive, complicated, and lengthy legal battles. Meanwhile, the death penalty continues to ignite fierce debate, questioning the very fabric of morality and justice. Consider this chapter an alarm clock for your conscience—a vivid illustration of how excessive penalties have escalated beyond the scale of the original crimes, often disproportionately affecting the less fortunate in society. It's high time we scrutinize the scales of justice to ensure they haven't tipped against the very principles they were designed to uphold.

Civil Litigation Under Fire The heart of the American legal system rests on the ability of an aggrieved person to seek justice in a court of law. The Seventh Amendment to the United States Constitution is clear in its intent: 'In Suits at common law, where the value in controversy shall exceed twenty dollars, the right of trial by jury shall be preserved.' Yet, the simplicity of this promise masks a contemporary landscape where civil litigation faces numerous challenges.

Consider the concept of 'access to justice.' It might sound like a given in a democracy, yet for many citizens, it's more of a mirage. Financial barriers stand like sentries at the courthouse doors. Lawyers' fees scare off those of modest means, and court costs pile high enough to dim the hopes of those fighting for redress or protection.

It's not just about money. The quagmire of procedural hurdles — motion after motion, complicated filing requirements, and Byzantine local rules — each acts as a tripwire to the uninitiated. Laypeople cringe at the thought of entering a legal fray not because their case lacks merit, but because the process seems so daunting, labyrinthine, and unforgiving.

Pause and think about the implications: when individuals can't seek corrective measures through civil lawsuits, the erosion of accountability takes place. Corporations, government institutions, and powerful entities operate with a decreased sense of consequence, knowing that the odds of being taken to task in court are slimming.

Class action lawsuits, a tool designed to empower the many against the few, are under siege. Through legislative and judicial actions, the threshold to form a class has been ratcheted higher. Even when classes are certified, settlements often provide minuscule payouts to individuals, questioning the efficacy of the process itself.

The issue at stake isn't trivial. Civil litigation is a cornerstone of dispute resolution in society and one of the chief mechanisms for citizens to enforce the laws and regulations designed to protect them. And yet, it's being chipped away, subtly reshaped to favor those already fortified with resources and influence.

A disturbing shift is manifesting in how disputes are resolved. Mandatory arbitration clauses are woven into consumer and employment contracts, insidiously stripping individuals of their right to a day in court. This trend nudges conflicts into the shadows, where arbitrators, not juries, deliver verdicts often in the absence of transparency and with a bias towards the contract drafter — usually companies or employers.

Now think about the notion of judicial independence, a bedrock principle for a functional system where civil claims can be heard and adjudicated fairly. But politics have permeated the judicial appointment process, so much so that the impartiality of the bench is questioned by many. Judges are human, but their robes come with the expectation of neutrality, regardless of the political winds blowing outside their chambers.

Each of these factors, alone, would be cause for alarm. Together, they signal a systematic weakening of one of the public's most potent legal protections. We are observing a pivotal moment where the ability for civil litigation to serve as an equalizing force is in jeopardy.

Why should this matter to you? Because today it's someone else's dispute, tomorrow it could be yours. Whether it's a conflict with an employer, a warranty ignored by a corporation, or harm caused by negligent behavior, the assurance that one can turn to the courts to make things right is foundational. It's not just your fight; it's our collective safeguard — a principle that stands guard over fairness and justice.

If acquiescence to this predicament is the response, the outcome is predictable. More barriers will materialize, more voices will be silenced, and the scales of justice will tilt further away from the grasp of the common citizen. However, if awareness sparks action, if knowledge fuels advocacy, then these patterns of restriction can be challenged, confronted, and corrected.

This moment calls for engagement; it beckons for a populace that won't stand by as their rights are curtailed and their powers diminished. Get informed about the procedures and the pitfalls. Learn how to navigate the landscape or support those fighting for systemic reform. Recognize the potent power of legislation and who writes it — and remember, those lawmakers are accountable to you. It's an exercise of citizenship to make your voice heard.

It won't be an overnight transformation. Systems, especially those as deep-rooted as our legal structure, evolve at a pace that can frustrate the most impassioned among us. But consider how the mightiest of barriers can be brought down by persistent, collective hammering at the cracks. Every effort to educate oneself, to engage in the process, and to cast a vote for justice, lodges a chisel into the wall that stands between people and their rights.

So, as we survey the challenges facing civil litigation, the call to arms is not one of physical conflict but of intellectual and civic engagement. Equip yourself with knowledge and fortitude. Stand in solidarity with those who seek fairness and remediation through our courts. It's not merely about protecting what we have; it's about reclaiming the promise of justice for all.

Take this knowledge, embrace the responsibility, and act with the conviction that a just society is not given but made, not assumed but ensured. This is your system, these are your rights, and this fight, this striving for a balanced scale, is undeniably yours.

The Death Penalty Debate emerges as a cardinal example of the friction between law and fundamental rights, and perhaps no other issue so starkly questions the morality, legality, and constitutionality of punishment. Within the sphere of the Eighth Amendment, the question arises: does capital punishment constitute "cruel and unusual" punishment, and thus infringe upon the constitutional rights of the individual?

The death penalty carries with it a weight that is both historical and deeply emotive. It casts long shadows over our understanding of justice, fairness, and humane treatment. Consider the process itself, where some accused may languish for years, a sword of Damocles hanging perpetually overhead, awaiting a fate sealed by the state. This process calls into question the very essence of due process and the promise of swift justice as articulated in the Sixth Amendment.

In dissecting the debate, we must recognize the divide between retribution and rehabilitation, two core philosophies at the heart of the criminal justice system. Those who endorse the death penalty often do so from a stance of deterrence and retribution, a view that some acts are so heinous they warrant the ultimate sanction. In contrast, the rehabilitation approach emphasizes the potential for change, arguing the state should not abandon hope for an individual's redemption.

Statistics and studies frequently enter the conversation, yet data can be as divisive as it is illuminating. While some research suggests that capital punishment does not successfully deter crime, proponents argue that the potential for a death sentence serves as a powerful deterrent against the most violent crimes. However, the chilling reality of wrongful executions – where new evidence surfaces too late – haunts the conscience, leaving irrevocable scars on our collective ethos.

The execution of justice demands consistency, yet the death penalty in practice is anything but uniform. Racial bias, socioeconomic disparity, and geographic arbitrariness paint a troubling picture. Justice must be blind, yet statistics reveal that it peeks all too often, with minorities and the disadvantaged disproportionately represented on death row.

Moreover, modern technology and forensic science have provided tools to revisit convictions with a level of scrutiny previously unimaginable. DNA testing has exonerated individuals who would have otherwise faced execution, suggesting that fallibility in the justice system can render permanent punishments a dangerous gamble with human lives.

Financial considerations also complicate the conversation. Some argue that the immense costs associated with capital cases, from trial to lengthy appeals to the actual execution, outweigh the financial burden of life imprisonment. Economics, then, challenge the practicality of the death penalty, urging us to count the cost, not only in moral terms but also in cold, hard currency.

The voices of victims' families must also be heard. Their tapestry of perspectives is as varied as it is poignant. Some find peace in the thought of an execution, while others vociferously advocate for abolition, finding no solace in the perpetuation of killing. Their pain reminds us that justice, although blind, must never be deaf to the cries of those who suffer in its wake.

International observations lend yet another layer to this debate. The global trend towards abolition of the death penalty shines a spotlight on the United States, often positioning it at odds with international human rights standards. This juxtaposition serves as a call to reexamine long-held practices against a broader backdrop of evolving norms.

Legal challenges persist, with cases regularly ascending to the highest courts in the land, prompting us to question and reassess the constitutional grounding of capital punishment. Each case serves as a crucible, refining our legal arguments and our deeper understanding of justice.

Addressing the death penalty is not an exercise in abstract law; it is an endeavor steeped in empathy, dignity, and a profound respect for life. As much as it is about those who have committed grave offenses, it is equally about who we are as a nation, the values we espouse, and the lengths we are willing to go to uphold them.

While we debate the death penalty, technology charges ever forward, bringing new methods of execution to the forefront. Lethal injection, viewed by some as a more humane method, has been scrutinized for botched procedures, prompting a reevaluation of what "humane" truly means in the context of taking a life.

Morality cannot be divorced from the law, and the death penalty debate extends into philosophical realms, questioning the very nature of existence and society's right to extinguish it. We come, then, to the heart of the battle between collective judgment and individual rights, each case prompting us to look within ourselves and determine the role of mercy in the face of unspeakable cruelty.

As this debate rages on, fueled by impassioned arguments on both sides, it becomes clear that the issue of the death penalty in America is not merely a policy to be measured, but a mirror reflecting our deepest beliefs about justice, equity, and the core values underpinning our constitutional framework.

In conclusion, the death penalty stands not just as a legal quandary, but as a beacon illuminating our most profound national conversations. It challenges us to ask difficult questions, to confront uncomfortable truths, and to pursue a justice that aligns with the unassailable rights endowed to every individual by the Constitution. As we contend with the weight of this debate, it is incumbent upon us to engage with the utmost care, unyielding integrity, and an unwavering commitment to the eternal principles of human dignity and constitutional sanctity.

The Rise of Excessive Penalties On the continuum of justice and liberty, there lies a tipping point where penalties designed to deter and punish cross the threshold into excess. This section forwards an urgent examination of the shift toward excessive penalties and their implications on individual rights. As our society grapples with maintaining order and upholding the law, questions arise: At what cost do these efforts come? How do they align with the values and protections enshrined in the Constitution? The Eighth Amendment, which guards against cruel and unusual punishment, appears to be fraying at the edges as the state exercises its punitive powers with unprecedented severity.

Within the pages of legislation and courtrooms, a subtle yet profound transformation is taking place. Financial sanctions, once a slap on the wrist, have ballooned into crippling debt for countless Americans. Meanwhile, prison sentences stretch on, often outlasting the context of the crimes they aim to punish. To understand this shift, one must look closely at the convergence of policy, societal expectations, and the often-unseen machinery of the legal system that turns the wheel of justice with an increasingly heavy hand.

A critical eye casts doubt on the justifications raised for these growing penalties. Do extreme sentences truly serve as effective deterrents, or do they rather reflect a punitive urge that overshadows the principles of rehabilitation and restitution? One cannot ignore the dual impact on both the individual and the collective conscience of a society that seems to regard ever-harsher consequences as the norm. The fabric of communal life frays when unchecked retribution overtakes reasoned response to wrongdoing.

Against a backdrop of escalating penalties, one must consider the stories of those entangled in this web of punitiveness. Lives upended by mandatory minimums, three-strikes laws, and habitual offender statutes – such narratives reveal a human element too often missing from policy debates. Disproportionate punishment not only undermines the individuals involved but also sows seeds of mistrust and division within communities. People see, feel, and ultimately question the balance of justice when punishment seems unmoored from the gravity of the crime.

Exploring the implications of these punitive excesses uncovers a troubling link to socioeconomic disparities. Marginalized communities bear a particularly heavy burden, with the weight of fines and long-term incarceration falling disproportionately on the shoulders of the poor and the less educated, accelerating cycles of poverty and disenfranchisement. These outcomes demand a rethinking of how society administers justice, prompting a push toward penalty reform and a recommitment to proportionality as a cornerstone of fair punishment.

Beneath the surface of these trends lies a deeper narrative concerning a criminal justice system operating at variance with its foundational purpose. When fines evolve into revenue-generating mechanisms for local governments or when prisons turn into de facto solution centers for social ills, the whole notion of punishment is distorted. Conflating financial solvency or the containment of societal problems with the administration of justice serves neither the interests of fairness nor the greater good. It is imperative to confront these deviations with conviction and to advocate for a return to principled justice.

In this context, one must also grapple with how policies such as asset forfeiture have expanded beyond their original remit. Originally intended to disrupt the financial infrastructure of organized crime, such measures have sometimes strayed, catching up ordinary citizens in a dragnet that assumes guilt and compels individuals to fight for the return of property undeservedly seized. This state of affairs has sparked a dialogue about due process and the presumption of innocence – fundamental tenets at risk of being overshadowed by the overzealous application of the law.

Amid a panorama of excessive penalties, some rays of hope shine through. Advocates for justice reform work tirelessly, challenging the status quo and driving legislative and judicial changes. Their mission is not only about mitigating the impact of current policies but also about reimagining a system that prioritizes transformation over punishment, healing over harm. This movement beckons society to aspire to a higher standard of justice and to remember the human capacity for change and recovery.

As critical reflection prompts action, evidence-based alternatives to excessive punishment emerge. Drug courts, restorative justice programs, and diversion initiatives illustrate successful strategies that move away from punitive excess and toward outcomes that support rehabilitation and social integration. The effectiveness of these approaches offers a powerful counterpoint to the prevailing winds of penalty and punishment, suggesting a path forward that can satisfy the demands of justice without resorting to draconian measures.

The pushback against such penalties is not just the task of lawyers, advocates, and policymakers; it is a calling for all citizens invested in the integrity of their justice system and the preservation of their constitutional rights. The challenge, then, is to engage with these issues thoughtfully and proactively, recognizing that the quality of mercy is not strained, nor is the pursuit of justice served by extremes. It is a civic duty to stand against the tide of excessive penalties and rally for reforms that reflect the values of fairness and humanity indelible in the American ethos.

Confronting the rise of excessive penalties, each individual must raise their voice, question the norm, and demand accountability. When the scales of justice tip too far, it is a collective responsibility to restore equilibrium. Indeed, the endurance of a nation's constitutional commitments is measured by its capacity to resist the encroachments of unchecked authority and to safeguard the liberties of its people against the creeping shadow of over-penalization.

The conversation surrounding excessive penalties cannot be relegated to the margins or silenced by the din of competing political narratives. It must take center stage in the public sphere as a matter of urgency and conscience. Amidst the relentless advance of legal penalties, this section shines an illuminating beacon, inviting transformation within a system in need of balance and beckoning a return to a justice both compassionate and appropriately measured.

By scrutinizing policies and practices that deviate from the core philosophies enshrined in the Constitution, society finds not only a cause for concern but also the impetus for change. The call that emanates from within these pages is for engagement, courage, and resolve in the pursuit of a justice system calibrated to the ideals of fairness and restraint. It rests upon the shoulders of every citizen to become a steward of the right to be free from excessive, cruel, and unusual punishment – a right that forms the bedrock of a dynamic and dignified democracy.

Chapter 9: Ninth and Tenth Amendments: The Forgotten Guarantees

As we turn the page on the previous chapters detailing the erosion of specific rights, we arrive at a critical yet often overlooked juncture—the Ninth and Tenth Amendments. These amendments serve as the guardians of our liberty, asserting the existence of fundamental rights beyond those explicitly listed and affirming the balance of power between the federal government and the states. They are the unspoken heroes, the reserves of democracy that protect against the overreach of federal authority and assure that our freedoms aren't hemmed in by the constraints of enumeration. It's a call to acknowledge that what isn't granted to Uncle Sam is reserved for the states, or more importantly, for you—the individual. When the interplay of laws and power dynamics tries to nudge us towards governmental dependency, these guarantees remind us that our Constitution isn't a finite list, but a beacon of empowerment for a people who value the boundless realm of unarticulated freedoms. This chapter isn't just about the Ninth and Tenth Amendments; it's a rallying cry to rediscover their seminal importance in our Constitutional framework and to champion their role in safeguarding the liberties that define our nation.

Unenumerated Rights and Their Disregard Amidst the often-cited articles and amendments of the U.S. Constitution lie aspects that, although equally crucial, are less prominently discussed and face an ever-increasing threat—the unenumerated rights under the Ninth Amendment. Acknowledging this, consider our blueprint of liberty not as a document of permissions but as one of inherent protections. These protections encompass rights not explicitly listed within the text, yet are fundamental to a free society and crucial to individual autonomy and dignity.

This section begins with the assertion that liberty is not confined to the written word. The Founders, sagacious in their foresight, perceived that no document could ever capture the full expanse of human freedoms. They understood that temporal and evolving societies would recognize new rights, contingencies they prepared for through the Ninth Amendment. Yet, despite this inclusivity, these unenumerated rights are overlooked, often overshadowed by the more prominently litigated rights within the Bill of Rights.

We live in times when personal autonomy on issues from parenting to medical decisions is being assailed. The mooring of our commitment to safeguarding individual freedoms is slipping as the executive, legislative, and judicial branches have collectively neglected those rights that the Constitution did not specifically enumerate. In the sweep of history, rights such as privacy have been established in landmark cases, yet today face new forms of intrusion and compromise as technological advances outpace legal protections.

One might argue that while enumerated rights draw distinct boundaries, unenumerated rights are riddled with ambiguity. This ambiguity, however, is not an excuse for their disregard but a call for vigilance in their defense. The contemporary era, replete with rapid technological development and evolving societal norms, demands that we revisit and reassert the value of these rights regularly to avoid erosion through ignorance or overreach.

Are we succumbing to convenience at the cost of our own freedoms? Let's look at how the surveillance state, under the guise of protection, chips away at the right to privacy—a right not specified in our Constitution, yet one that forms the bedrock of individual security and freethinking. Through data mining, location tracking, and mass interception of communications, a once-unimaginable reach into personal lives has become commonplace, and the question remains: have we unknowingly consented to this invasion?

The disregard isn't merely an issue of passive erosion; it's one of active disenfranchisement. Take, for example, the restriction of personal freedom when it comes to practices outside the mainstream. Cultural and spiritual expressions that deviate from the norm are discouraged, sometimes legally impeded, despite the Founders' implicit protection of such personal liberations.

When unchecked authority presses its will upon the people, we see the raw power of government restraining the ingenuity and creativity of its constituency. Actions taken in the name of safety or morality, without the liege of the courts' protection of unstated rights, threaten the core of our republic's philosophy. Each individual's liberty to pursue their vision of happiness is sacred, a notion that needs reiteration and robust defense in contemporary times.

In confronting these challenges, history is our oracle. It forewarns us about the paths nations can tread when governments dismiss the unseen boundaries of individual liberty. The unenumerated rights are not relics of a past age but beacons for current and future generations. They represent freedom whose essence is understood universally through the human condition—not solely through the lens of American jurisprudence.

In addressing the political tightrope, one must concede that balance is delicate. Indeed, governance requires powers to regulate for the common good, yet these must not become chains that bind the free will and mute the vibrant expression of its people. As citizens, our watch guard is eternal vigilance, our compass, the founding principles that echo from the age of enlightenment into the digital era.

The resurgence of attention to these rights in our public discourse and legal arenas is imperative. Our country's judiciary must remain a haven for justice, weighing the silent rights alongside the vocalized. In this pursuit, the courts must illuminate the penumbra, the shadows where these rights lie, and bring them into the spectrum of legitimate debate and legal recognition.

Consider action as the virtue in waiting. We must involve ourselves, whether through education, discourse, or direct advocacy, to ensure these rights are not cast aside. Our contemporary quandaries are not novel in theme but in form, and thus demand a revitalized commitment to principles that sustain the human spirit and foster its growth.

So where does this leave us, as inheritors of freedoms that must be actively curated and defended? It places us at the exact moment where we must recognize the interplay between vigilance and liberty, understanding that the rights won by our forebearers must be continually affirmed, articulated, and zealously guarded in our time. It's incumbent upon us, the living embodiment of our nation's ideals, to ensure they survive in more than just parchment and proclamation.

To achieve this lofty yet attainable goal, education is the weapon of choice, understanding the law, not as a tool for those with robed authority alone but as the common heritage of every citizen. Together, this enriched understanding becomes our shield, a bulwark against the tide of oversight and oblivion that faces the unenumerated rights that are the breath of our nation's soul.

Thus, we march forward, not in settled complacency, but with the firm stride of those who build, maintain, and defend the grand structure of liberty. Not merely for oneself but for all, ensuring that the rights unnamed retain their vigor and place within our collective heart, now and ever onwards.

States' Rights Versus Federal Overreach

The fabric of American democracy is woven with a delicate balance between the states and the federal government—a balance predicated on autonomy and unity. Both were envisioned to coexist, to complement, not to compete. Yet, history has illustrated a pendulum swing in this balance, tipping at times toward federal dominance. This section delves into the tension between states' rights and federal overreach, unveiling instances where the scales may not tip but instead slam down against the constitutional promise of reserved powers to the states.

The Ninth and Tenth Amendments serve as the bulwarks for states' rights, explicitly affirming that the powers not delegated to the United States by the Constitution, nor prohibited by it to the states, are reserved to the states respectively, or to the people. But these declarations, clear in their wording, face challenges from broad interpretations of other constitutional provisions—leading to debates and decisions that often enhance federal power at the expense of the states.

Consider the implication of the Commerce Clause, which has served as one of the primary conduits for expanding federal influence. Ostensibly, it grants Congress the power to regulate commerce among the several states, but over time, this clause has been interpreted to affect virtually any activity with even the most tenuous link to economic behavior. This broad view chips away at the sovereignty promised to states, giving rise to a central government with reach into nearly all aspects of governance.

Moreover, federal funding comes with strings attached—often in the form of regulations that states must follow to receive such funds. Thus, federal overreach isn't always direct but frequently comes veiled as conditional generosity. States find themselves in a bind, compelled to comply with policies that may not reflect their citizens' preferences or put their unique needs into account due to the lure or necessity of federal financial support.

One can't ignore the expansive role of the federal judicial branch either, particularly the Supreme Court, in interpreting state laws alongside federal laws. Whenever there's a conflict of interest, supremacy has historically favored the national legislature, even when outcomes may silence the states' distinct voices, undermining their ability to govern as closer representatives of their citizenry.

Environmental regulations present yet another consistent battlefield. The federal determination to set a uniform standard often clashes with states' appeals for autonomy in modulating their resources. While a single national standard simplifies regulation, it neglects the reality that each state faces unique environmental challenges. Consequently, states are forced into a one-size-fits-all solution that may not be ideal—or even effective—for their specific context.

The crux of the conflict often tilts on the axis of political ideology as well. Certain factions push for a stronger central government to promote uniformity and national standards, while others advocate for resilience within states, claiming that state governments better approximate the needs and values of their constituents than a distant federal authority.

This friction isn't merely a political conundrum but also a reflection of diverse philosophies about governance. The debate taps into fundamental questions about the nature of our union: Is it a collective of quasi-sovereign states or a single entity with distributed administrative districts?

To scrutinize the current landscape, one must also analyze the elasticity of federal power in emergencies. National crises, whether economic, health-related, or security-based, provide grounds for the federal government to temporarily amass and exercise exceptional power. However, the generational challenge emerges when temporary becomes seemingly permanent, constraining states' ability to recoup their legislative and executive privileges.

Additionally, the creeping federal influence over education distorts the division of authority. While states traditionally presided over their educational systems, we've witnessed increased federal intrusion—via mandates, standardized testing, and curriculum influences—that questions whether the promise of state-run education has eroded under the weight of national standardization.

Moving from education to health care, the Affordable Care Act, also colloquially known as Obamacare, provides a contemporary case study. The act's implementation hinged upon the contentious debate over states' roles in managing health care and whether the federal imposition was an unjustifiable intrusion into the domain traditionally overseen by states.

Immigration policies add further complexity. As a theoretically exclusive federal jurisdiction, states chafe at their lack of input, especially when undocumented immigrants significantly impact their resources and communities. The interweaving of local law enforcement in implementing federal immigration laws demonstrates an overlap that many argue should be carefully recalibrated to honor states' rights.

Drug policy, particularly the legalization of marijuana, is an evident tableau of this dichotomy. States that have legalized its use operate in defiance of federal law, which still classifies marijuana as an illegal substance. This puts citizens and local businesses in a precarious position— caught between adherence to state law and potential federal penalties.

Envisaging a pathway forward requires balance, dialogue, and a steadfast commitment to founding principles. Federal overreach needs to be recognized, not as an abstract political term but as a tangible encroachment on individual liberties and the rightful domain of state governance. Moreover, states must navigate a course that respects the union while advocating for their prerogatives.

It's crucial then, in seeking to uphold the Constitution and the freedoms it safeguards, to address the increasing diluted nature of states' rights in the shadow of federal overreach. Redrawing the lines that define federal and state powers is perhaps one of the most pressing crusades for upholding the constitutional architecture of the United States. Reflect on this: Does an overreaching federal government truly serve the people, or does it undermine the very cornerstone of our democratic republic?

Chapter 10: The War on Terror and Constitutional Erosion

Emerging from the shadows of history's gravest attacks, a nation resolved that security shall not be compromised, unwittingly stood at the precipice of constitutional erosion. 'The War on Terror', a phrase that resonated with the promise of protection, became a veil for the subtle, yet significant, loss of the very liberties it vowed to safeguard. Vigilance turned to infringement as the line between liberty and security blurred—detention without trial no longer a narrative in dystopian fiction, but a reality challenging the constructs of a civil justice system. A state of perpetual conflict gave rise to a milieu where the military's reach extended into realms once safeguarded by civilian oversight, setting a precedent that threatens the bedrock of American jurisprudence. As this era unfolds, complacency cannot be the citizen's refuge; awareness must spark action, for in the struggle to reclaim the delicate balance between rights and security lies the true essence of freedom's endurance.

Sacrificing Liberty for Security? When faced with the complex and challenging landscape of safeguarding a nation, it is a seductive trade-off to exchange freedoms for the promise of security. This section navigates through the treacherous waters where liberty and safety seemingly clash, illuminating a path that honors both without diminishing either.

In the wake of existential threats, primarily those categorized under the vast umbrella of terrorism, governments often enact measures designed to stiffen security at the expense of individual freedoms. The rationale is understandable, but the execution can tip the scales away from the protections enshrined in the Constitution.

Consider the narrative that has unfolded since the onset of the War on Terror. Laws and policies, often rushed through the legislative process, have ostensibly targeted the preservation of life and property, yet in doing so, they've encroached upon the liberty they're meant to defend. It's essential to ask ourselves whether the cost to our civil liberties mirrors the benefits of these security measures.

The Patriot Act exemplifies this dilemma. Hastily enacted in the aftermath of a national tragedy, it expanded governmental powers to survey and detain. Its provisions, while arguably protective, harbor the potential for abuse. Critics argue that certain sections, intended to sunset, persist today, indicating a perpetuity that does not align with the temporary nature of the threats they address.

Engagement in proactive security should not be anathema to civil liberty. Yet, history is pockmarked with instances where the veil of national security masks the erosion of individual rights. Through surveillance programs and data collection, the line between personal privacy and public safety blurs, leaving a residue of suspicion and potential for exploitation.

Take, for instance, the battleground of encryption and data privacy. Measures to combat cyberterrorism have frequently clashed with the right to privacy in communications. While it's crucial to thwart malicious actors, doing so shouldn't require stripping down the digital safeguards that also protect law-abiding citizens.

A delicate balance is imperative. There exists a profound difference between implementing security measures with transparency and oversight and adopting sweeping surveillance powers under the guise of protection. When the latter occurs, citizens' trust in their government erodes, which is antithetical to the ethos of democracy.

The relevance of this balance resounds in the discussion over detention practices. Holding individuals indefinitely without trial in the name of national security contravenes the core legal principles upon which the United States was founded. Habeas corpus, the right to challenge unlawful detention, is not a casualty of war but a survivor of it.

Furthermore, security should not be a carte blanche rationale for military action on domestic soil. The principle of posse comitatus, which prohibits military involvement in civilian law enforcement, exists for this precise reason. It safeguards against the military becoming an oppressive force against the population it's intended to protect.

Examining executive orders through the lens of security illustrates the thin boundary between vital responsive action and executive overreach. While decisive responsiveness to threats is a presidential prerogative, abiding by Constitutional constraints is non-negotiable.

Yet, amid this landscape of trade-offs, there are shining examples of harmonious security and liberty. Civilian oversight committees, for one, have demonstrated the potential to serve as the guardians at the gates of freedom, carefully scrutinizing actions taken in the name of security to ensure that they do not infringe on rights unduly.

It's also worth noting that the strength of a nation's security apparatus doesn't come solely from its capacity to restrict and surveil; it emerges from the resilience of its free citizens. Safety born from fear is a hollow imitation of security. Genuine protection fosters empowerment and respects dignity.

So, where does this leave us? It's a reminder that vigilance is required, not solely against external threats but against the internal creep of authoritarian practices under the auspice of securing safety. Each instance where liberty is offered as a sacrifice must be scrutinized with unyielding intensity. Every measure must be weighed on the scales of justice and history. As court cases and legislative battles shape the contours of this debate, it's the citizen's voice that must ring loudest.

Security and liberty must not stand in opposition but rather converge like tributaries to a great river, each reinforcing the other. Absolute security is an illusion, as is absolute freedom, but in their balanced dance, we find the essence of a society that thrives.

This conversation does not stop here, nor should it ever. A nation's narrative is not static, and the discussion regarding liberty in the face of security must continue to evolve. As new challenges arise, so too must new solutions that maintain the integrity of the very freedoms that define a nation worth securing. This is the challenge before us, and the mantle of responsibility now lies squarely on the shoulders of each individual. It's time to redefine what it means to be secure by ensuring that liberty is not the price paid but the principle protected.

Detention Without Trial: A New Norm? Powerful questions grip our society as we confront the challenges to the Constitution in the post-9/11 era. Central to these concerns is the treatment of individuals in the context of national security and the troubling trend of detention without trial. This issue not just tests the principles of due process but also stands as a litmus for the resilience of our constitutional rights.

It's easy to feel disconnected from the layers of policy and law that wrap around cases of detention without trial, but to understand our rights, we must dive deep into the murky waters of legal precedent and policy that shape this reality. When the government justifies the indefinite detention of individuals on security grounds, it pulls at the very fabric of the constitutional promise of liberty and justice for all.

Consider the historical safeguards of the Sixth Amendment: the right to a speedy and public trial, by an impartial jury. These rights have been fixtures of American justice since the earliest days of our republic. Yet, in recent times, these guarantees seem to waver under the weight of national security concerns, leaving many to wonder if due process is itself becoming a relic.

The post-9/11 security apparatus introduced legislation that enabled scenarios where individuals could be held without charge. The imagery of Guantanamo Bay, for instance, evokes a landscape where rights are suspended in the shadow of security. It compels us to scrutinize whether the fear of what might be outweighs the fundamental rights that define who we are.

Detention without trial disrupts the narrative of a just society and poses profound ethical questions. How do we measure the cost of such actions? What are the invisible lines crossed when we allow the indefinite suspension of basic rights? These are not questions with easy answers, but they demand a reckoning if we are to uphold the spirit of the Constitution.

Detention policies also have a ripple effect, cementing a precedent that could be used against anyone deemed a threat, often without transparent criteria. This is not just about those currently detained—it casts all citizens in a potential net of suspicion without the assurance of due process.

Transparency and accountability seem to lose their significance in the context of these detentions. The practice implies a willingness to bypass the judiciary, the very system designed to protect citizens from arbitrary power. If the bedrock of justice can be circumvented in the name of national security, where does that leave the individual?

It is crucial for citizens to confront this new norm, not through violence or blind anger, but through informed, tenacious demand for due process. This requires engagement with our legal systems, and insistence that legislation adhere to the Constitution.

The rule of law cannot be a fair-weather friend, discarded when convenience dictates. Its sustainability rests on its application in times of peace and crisis alike. When laws that subvert the basic tenets of fair treatment arise, it is the duty of the citizen to take a firm but lawful stand against them.

Imagine a society where detention without trial becomes commonplace. How swiftly the pillars of freedom could crumble, leaving in their wake a system unrecognizable to the founders. It is the task of the current generation to question, challenge, and reverse the tide that threatens to redefine these norms.

We must demand mechanisms of oversight and reform that prevent the slide into complacency and complicity that allows such practices to continue. Every instance of detention without trial should be examined with the utmost scrutiny, and the rationale behind it laid bare for public discourse.

Resilience in the face of fear is a hallmark of courage. It is time to show that courage by demanding a standard of justice that does not bend to the whim of panic. Our nation's history is rich with examples of individuals who stood for what was constitutionally right, often against overwhelming odds. It is in this tradition that today's citizens must stand.

Detention without trial stands not as an isolated issue but as a symptom of a broader struggle for constitutional integrity. There is a line between protecting a nation and protecting the civil liberties that define it. Knowing where that line lies, and defending it, is the charge of every citizen.

To remain vigilant is to embody the spirit of the Constitution. We must hold fast to the principles of due process and rule of law, particularly when they are most under threat. If detention without trial becomes a new norm, it will not be because our Constitution has failed us, but because we have failed it.

Let's reflect on the stark reality that the fabric of our justice system is entrusted to our collective care. Our collective voice must resonate in courts, in legislative chambers, and in public squares, always remembering the power and responsibility we have to shape the future of our Constitution and our country.

The Military Versus Civil Justice Systems It takes a certain type of courage to scrutinize the mechanisms of justice, particularly when peeling back the layers of military versus civil systems. At first glance, they may seem worlds apart, designed to address entirely unique landscapes of legality. Yet upon closer examination, one uncovers the inevitable friction between the two, friction that often gives rise to questions about the rights of citizens and the extent of government control.

Our nation's history is deeply rooted in the commitment to civilian oversight and due process. This commitment is the foundation upon which civil justice systems were built. In parallel, the creation of military justice systems served the pragmatic need to maintain order within the armed forces, separate from the civilian realm. Both essential, yet distinctively different in practice and philosophy.

One traverses the civil justice landscape to find a system teeming with the checks and balances of democratic governance. It's a realm where principles of transparency and accountability are not just expected but required. Trials are public, the right to an attorney is inviolable, and juries of one's peers sit in judgement, upholding the fabric of fair play woven through the Constitution.

Turning to military justice, however, reveals a framework that operates under a different set of prerogatives. Military courts are governed by the Uniform Code of Military Justice (UCMJ), setting standards deeply intertwined with the unique demands of military service. These courts address conduct detrimental to the unity and effectiveness of military personnel, and as such, are adjudicated swiftly, often behind the closed doors of hierarchy and command.

Imagine for a moment the solitary figure of a soldier facing a court-martial panel. The composition of the panel starkly contrasts with a jury of one's peers that one expects in a civil courtroom. While the fidelity to justice is a common purpose, the paths to its delivery markedly diverge. The soldier answers to superiors vested with the authority to discipline within the ranks. This is a necessity of military life, where cohesion often dictates the margin between life and death.

In the shadow of a post-9/11 world, the lines that once clearly delineated military discipline from civil liberties have blurred. The War on Terror introduced a new dynamic, where individuals, often civilians, could be labeled 'enemy combatants' and thereby subjected to military jurisdiction, eschewing the civil rights guaranteed in the Constitution. A troubling precedent for suspending habeas corpus and denying access to civil courts emerged from this new dynamic.

The military commissions established in Guantanamo Bay serve as a stark example. Detainees, bereft of the full legal protections accorded in civil courts, find themselves in a legal limbo. The commissions underscore a departure from the principles of openness, pivoting towards secrecy and efficiency. This pivot raises alarms for those who hold the Constitution not only as the supreme law of the land but as the incorruptible guardian of liberties.

Consider this. When a civilian is accused of a crime, the architecture of justice demands that they receive a trial, where evidence is weighed, and due process clings to them like a shield. But this shield can be sidestepped by drawing upon legislative instruments such as the Authorization for Use of Military Force (AUMF), which can expand the military's role in detaining individuals without the customary safeguards of the Bill of Rights.

It can be argued that such measures are in response to modern threats that do not fit neatly into a peacetime paradigm of justice. Yet, each step down this path is a step away from the constitutional promise. To echo a vital question — when we temper liberties in the name of security, what are the greater risks?

Diligence in the protection of our constitutional guarantees is essential. We must be vigilant, standing guard over not only the rights we exercise daily but also over those that lie dormant until moments of peril awaken their necessity. It's not merely about having protections on paper; it's about ensuring they endure the storms of security crises.

In facing the challenges between preserving public safety and guarding constitutional rights, we must reflect deeply. Our reflection compels us to recognize that the principles of justice — fairness, impartiality, and the right to be heard — are not the exclusive domain of civilian life but are equally esteemed within the military sphere, albeit adapted to its reality.

Empowering the populous with an understanding of this balance is no small task, yet it is undeniably critical. A population informed about the nuances that distinguish military and civil justice systems is better equipped to engage in discourse and decision-making that shapes the future of our rights and freedoms.

The resilience of the United States Constitution depends on its citizens' resolve to preserve its tenets. It requires a boldness to question, a willingness to engage and the fortitude to demand accountability from those who govern, regardless of the banner under which justice is served.

As we approach the juncture where national security interfaces with individual freedoms, the discourse must remain robust. These discussions set the stage for pivotal decisions that will either fortify or fracture the constitutional safeguard of liberties. It invites citizens to play an active role in the preservation of justice in all its forms.

Ultimately, the nexus between the military and civil systems of justice is where the enduring strength of our Constitution is tested. As citizens, we anchor ourselves to the promise that our rights are inalienable, a promise held in trust for every generation. That we have the resolve to defend that promise against encroachment is the litmus test of our nation's fidelity to the rule of law.

Chapter 11: The Judicial Branch: Activism vs. Restraint

The pendulum of justice swings between activism and restraint, a dynamic that shapes the liberties and lives of citizens. Within the hallowed halls of the judiciary, the balance of power is a tightrope walked with utmost care. Our guardians of the Constitution, the courts, play a pivotal role, and when they stumble into activism or err on the side of restraint, the very fabric of our democracy trembles. As we peer into the labyrinth of the Supreme Court's controversies and the far-reaching influence of the lower courts, we unveil the subtle, yet profound, ways in which policy is shaped, setting precedents that reverberate across generations. It's essential to scrutinize the checks and balances that are designed to prevent overstepping, to understand where they hold firm and where they falter. This chapter is not just about legal concepts; it's an appeal to the core of American values and a call to every citizen to seek a judiciary that speaks not through political voices, but through the immortal declarations of our Constitution.

Supreme Court Controversies

The Supreme Court, the highest judicial power in the United States, is not immune to controversy. Its decisions often reverberate through every layer of American life, shaping the legal landscape for generations. At its core, the Court's role is to interpret the Constitution, but sometimes, these interpretations deeply divide the nation, challenging our collective understanding of what the Constitution stands for.

Consider cases that touch on hot-button issues: abortion, affirmative action, campaign finance, and the rights of the accused. Each decision on these topics generates headlines, provokes public debate, and, at times, leads to questions about the Court's position in American democracy. Moreover, rulings can crystallize into flashpoints, symbolizing broader societal rifts and fueling disputes about judicial overreach or abdication of responsibility.

The appointment process has become a political battlefield. Enduring, lifetime appointments mean that each seat carries immense influence. The vetting of nominees is now a spectacle that reflects partisan divides, with question marks over the impartiality and integrity of the process. When the composition of the Court appears ideologically skewed, faith in its ability to act as a neutral arbiter diminishes.

Some assert that the Court has strayed far from its intended purpose, taking an active role in policy making rather than simply interpreting law. Critics worry when the Court strikes down legislation or establishes new legal standards; seeing this as stepping on the legislature's toes. Yet, supporters argue it's within the Court's prerogative to ensure laws adhere to the nation's founding principles.

Historic decisions can transport the Court into the center of controversies. Take Roe v. Wade, for instance, which anchored a woman's right to an abortion within the right to privacy. Decades later, the topic remains a battlefield with the Court's every word and indication parsed by activists, lobbyists, and politicians on both sides of the issue.

Recent trends suggest increasing polarization among the justices themselves. Decisions are often split along perceived ideological lines, leading to skepticism about the Court being above partisan politics. This perception is particularly pronounced when cases of significant political consequence, like Bush v. Gore, come before the Court.

Another area of Supreme Court controversy concerns the matter of judicial activism versus judicial restraint. Accusations fly of judges legislating from the bench, specifically in cases where they appear to create, rather than interpret, the law. In such instances, the debate intensifies over whether the justices are respecting the Constitution or molding it to fit their views.

The interpretation of the Constitution is expected to evolve, reflecting changes in society and norms. Yet, some argue that this malleability opens the door for justices to inject personal biases into their rulings, which begs the question: how much innovation is too much before it distorts the original intent of the framers?

Citizens keen on understanding their rights under the Constitution look at the Court's rulings as guideposts. When those decisions are cloaked in controversy, it becomes challenging to discern stable legal ground. As subjects of the law, it's incumbent upon us to scrutinize these rulings, deliberate their implications, and converse about whether they serve the collective good.

One can't discuss Supreme Court controversies without delving into the dissents. These alternative perspectives, often overshadowed by the majority opinion, can provide insightful critiques, reflect the zeitgeist of the times, and even influence future legal thought.

A dynamic tension exists between the Court's decisions and public sentiment. When the Court seems out of step with prevailing societal views, it triggers a complex debate about the role of judiciary in shaping or responding to public opinion. Should the Court lead the pack or follow democratically expressed will?

The Supreme Court's mandate is unequivocal; to interpret the Constitution. Yet it operates in a fabric of shifting societal values and political tides. Navigating such waters necessitates transparency and a clear rationale for its decisions, ensuring that every American can follow the logic that underpins the Supreme Court's role in our Republic.

Each controversy also offers a learning opportunity. Analyzing the intricacies of these judicial disagreements hones our understanding of the law and the Constitution's principles. It reinforces the importance of an engaged citizenry in holding public institutions accountable, ensuring they work for the public interest.

Facing a Supreme Court controversy calls for a dual approach: a commitment to seeking out information and a willingness to engage in the difficult conversations that follow. It is through this engagement that the Constitution remains a living document, relevant and responsive to the people it governs.

In the grand scheme, Supreme Court controversies aren't mere legal squabbles; they're vital, democratic dialogues that shape our nation's direction. They compel us to reflect on our values, question our assumptions, and, ultimately, participate in the enduring task of defining what America stands for. As we turn each page of history, let us remember the words of Justice Louis Brandeis: "The most important political office is that of the private citizen."

The Role of Lower Courts in Shaping Policy

In the intricate dance of checks and balances, history tends to shine the spotlight on the Supreme Court. Yet, it's often overlooked that lower courts play a critical role in shaping the policies that affect daily life. Their courtrooms are where the abstract of the Constitution becomes tangible, where law is not just pronounced but also practiced. These courts set the scene for local precedent, steering policy in significant and often unrealized ways.

Understanding the extent of lower court influence requires an appreciation for their sheer volume. Across the land, thousands of federal judges conduct the business of the judiciary, far from the gaze that scrutinizes their colleagues on the nation's highest bench. In these courts, policy is shaped quietly but effectively, case by case.

The process begins with interpretation. Every phrase in the Constitution can be distilled into a multitude of meanings; it's the job of lower court judges to decide which interpretation applies at any given moment. This shapes policy by influencing how broader laws are enforced. Take, for instance, the Fourth Amendment protections against unreasonable searches—every interpretation that upholds or questions the legality of a search impacts the policy surrounding individual rights and law enforcement tactics.

When groups seek to challenge or affirm legislation, their first battles are often in district courts. Here, judges' rulings can kickstart policy changes long before the Supreme Court weighs in—if it ever does. In matters ranging from immigration to environmental regulations, district courts serve as test beds for legal arguments that could redefine policy.

Moreover, circuit courts of appeal hold immense sway, standardizing legal interpretations across multiple states. Their rulings send a clear message about which policies will likely stand and which will falter under constitutional scrutiny. Through this, they set precedent that lower courts, in turn, adhere to or challenge.

It's crucial to recognize that these courts also serve as gatekeepers for the Supreme Court. They decide which matters are settled firmly enough to not require further review and which will ascend to higher judicial scrutiny. This function places them at a strategic point in the policy-shaping process, determining not just the flow of legal discourse but its very content.

The idea of 'case law' or 'common law' further underlines the influence of these judicial bodies. Developed over centuries, this framework relies heavily on past decisions to guide the outcomes of current cases. Thus, every ruling by a lower court judge weaves a new thread into the rich tapestry of our legal system, setting standards that govern future policy on every level.

What's more, the decentralized nature of lower courts means their rulings can mirror the diverse values and perspectives of the regions they serve. This patchwork of policy influences can sometimes push the national conversation forward when local rulings ignite broader movements for change.

In matters of civil rights, for example, it has often been the bold decisions from lower courts that catalyze transformative policy shifts. Immigration issues, including the fraught policy around Dreamers, often see their fate molded in court decisions long before reaching a national consensus. These courts, therefore, become arenas where societal values and legal principles battle for prominence.

One might also consider the implications of courts on electoral policy. Legal battles concerning gerrymandering and voter suppression tactics frequently unfold in the domain of lower courts. Their verdicts can have far-reaching consequences on who has access to the democratic process and whose voices are amplified or silenced.

Federal magistrate judges, who initially deal with issues like pretrial hearings or bail decisions, also wield policy influence. Their judgments can highlight systemic issues, such as the need for bail reform or changes in sentencing guidelines - acting as catalysts for policy review and reform.

Administrative law judges play their part too, presiding over specialized cases that involve federal regulations and agencies. Their rulings define the scope of agency power and the extent to which individuals and businesses can push back against regulatory controls. In essence, they're at the forefront of shaping policy that balances governmental authority with individual liberties.

The pace at which policies change can be directly attributed to the rapidly evolving decisions within the lower courts. It's a dynamic environment, one where rulings issued today can be tested against new standards tomorrow, responding to the changing mores of society, technology, and legal understanding.

In the fight for upholding constitutional rights, lower courts often stand as the first line of defense. It is within their jurisdiction that the most immediate and accessible justice is dispensed. Their interpretation of laws and rights therefore has a compounding effect on the policies that govern and protect citizens' freedoms.

In summary, while the limelight often falls on the Supreme Court, it's the unsung role of lower courts that continuously carves the contours of policy. These courts are where legal battles are fought and won, long before issues make it to the headlines or reach the apex of the judicial pyramid. Their decisions may not always capture the public imagination, but their impact reverberates through the arteries of the legal system, shaping policy in profound and enduring ways.

As citizens, understanding the influence of lower courts empowers us to better navigate and engage with the policies that frame our rights. It instills a recognition that each court decision, regardless of attention it receives, is a building block in the ever-evolving edifice of freedom and justice.

Checks, Balances, and Overstepping Boundaries

In illuminating the shadows cast by governmental overreach, it's crucial we grasp the mechanisms meant to prevent such occurrences: checks and balances. The U.S. Constitution didn't just create a blueprint for government; it established a system to keep each branch in line, ensuring one does not overpower the others or the people. Here, we dive into how checks and balances function and the moments they fail, allowing overstepping boundaries.

The legislative, executive, and judicial branches possess distinct powers, yet they can challenge each other. For instance, the President may veto a law, but Congress can override this veto with a two-thirds majority vote. This interplay should keep tyrannical inclinations in check. However, there have been instances where one branch extends its reach, diminishing the effectiveness of this model.

When the judiciary takes on an activist role, interpreting the Constitution in ways that exponentially expand its own influence, it tiptoes on the edge of its jurisdiction. This encroachment can happen subtly, through decisions that set far-reaching precedents, which in turn can end up reshaping societal norms without going through the legislative process.

The executive branch, through the use of executive orders and national emergencies, has also been guilty of stretching its constitutional remit. Often justified under times of crisis, these actions can set dangerous precedents. When power is asserted unchecked, liberty hangs in the balance, and the very foundations of democratic governance are threatened.

Congress, the body directly elected to represent the people, is not immune to overstepping. Through sweeping regulations and laws that lack clarity, it can inadvertently grant too much power to the executive agencies charged with interpreting these laws. The result? A bloated bureaucracy that operates with little oversight and accountability.

Another concern is the habitual funding of programs through omnibus spending bills, which often contain measures that have not been thoroughly debated or even read by most lawmakers. This process can perpetuate unchecked growth in government size and spending, sidestepping the more deliberate, piecemeal legislative scrutiny the framers intended.

The balance of power is delicate, and its preservation demands perpetual vigilance. But when boundaries are overstepped, it's not just a political misstep—it's a direct affront to the principles enshrined in the Constitution. This leads to a pivotal question: What are the consequences when checks and balances are ignored, and how does this impact your constitutional rights?

One consequence is the potential erosion of individual liberties. If the executive branch oversteps and encroaches on civil liberties in the name of national security, it can lead to practices like unwarranted surveillance or detention without trial. Similarly, if the legislative branch passes laws that overly restrict freedoms in the guise of public safety, the personal freedoms guaranteed by the Bill of Rights can be imperiled.

An activist judiciary, meanwhile, can alter the landscape of rights without a single vote cast by the people or their representatives. By interpreting laws in ways that stretch beyond their original intent, the judicial branch can reduce the direct influence citizens have on the rules that govern them. Moreover, it can create a shadow legislation, where judicial precedents carry the weight of laws without the democratic foundation.

Transparency suffers when checks and balances are undermined. The more the branches of government blur their boundaries and extend their reach, the more opaque and confusing their actions become to the average citizen. This lack of clarity diminishes trust and makes it harder for individuals to understand, let alone challenge, government actions.

The defining characteristic of a functioning democracy is the ability of its institutions to self-correct, to return to a state of equilibrium when they have extended beyond their mandated powers. Yet, as history shows, this reversion to balance is not always automatic or forthcoming. It often requires concerted effort from engaged and informed citizens who are willing to call out and stand up against unconstitutional expansions.

In confronting the encroachments on constitutional rights, what can be done? It begins with education. A thorough understanding of what powers each branch has, what checks are in place, and the historical context in which overreaches have occurred is paramount. Action must follow awareness, with citizens raising their voices, whether through voting, litigation, or peaceful demonstration.

Civic engagement is the catalyst. When people demonstrate their investment in the workings of their government, elected officials and public servants take notice. The court of public opinion can exert immense pressure on the branches of government to adhere to their constitutional limits and responsibilities, reducing the likelihood of overreach. Yet, this can only happen if citizens remain ever-watchful, ever-questioning, and ever-prepared to take action.

Finally, it's important to remember the power of precedents. When a boundary is overstepped without consequence, it sets a norm. Each unconstitutional act that goes unchallenged weakens the foundation of our liberties. Therefore, challenging these precedents, through legal avenues, public discourse, and political activism, is not just your right—it's your responsibility.

Checks and balances are not self-executing mechanisms; they require the fuel of an engaged and informed electorate to function as intended. Each time a branch of government attempts to overstep its boundaries, it's an opportunity for citizens to stand firm, remind those in power of the Constitution's authority, and reinforce the separations that safeguard freedom. This is not solely the domain of politicians and judges—it's the arena where every American has a stake, where every American can make a difference.

Chapter 12: Executive Power: When Presidents Push Limits

Leapfrogging from the judiciary's delicate dance between activism and restraint, we pivot to explore a realm where the Constitution teeters on a tightrope of interpretation—the Executive branch. Here power pulsates, beckoning presidents to the siren call of unilateral action. *Executive Power: When Presidents Push Limits* scrutinizes the kaleidoscope of measures draped in the banner of urgency or necessity. Sometimes shrouded in secrecy, other times bold, presidential actions have tested the tether of constitutional permissions. In these pages, we unravel the complex fabric of executive orders, the wielding of national emergencies to extend authority, and the controversial embrace of the unitary executive theory. By piercing through the haziness of power's provenance, we uncover not only how but why presidents have stretched their sanctioned scope. As defenders of democracy, it's vital to scrutinize and question these presidential precedents with tenacity equal to the trust we place in our leaders. For it's within this vigilance that liberty finds its fiercest guardians.

A History of Executive Orders has been a pivotal element within the American political landscape. At their core, these powerful tools emerge directly from the Constitution, coupling strength with the stroke of a pen, and they have shaped the nation we inhabit today. The narrative of executive orders is neither black nor white; it's awash with the colors of necessity, ambition, and controversy. These orders, innate to the executive branch, grant Presidents the ability to direct and manage operations within the federal government, yet they were not explicitly defined in the early years of our Constitution.

Delving into the origins, the term 'executive order' has no formal definition in our founding document. It is from the implicit powers vested in the President by Article II of the Constitution that they derive their reach and consequence. Initially, these orders were infrequent and often mundane, but they have blossomed into tools of profound change, capable of repaving the societal landscape overnight, courting both acclaim and scrutiny.

The legacy of executive orders arguably begins with George Washington, who utilized such proclamations to establish protocols and assert presidential authority in a manner that was inchoate, testing the boundaries of his newly-inherited office. It was, however, during times of war and tumult that executive orders found their most expansive and impactful use. Abraham Lincoln's Emancipation Proclamation, issued during the fiery crucible of the Civil War, serves as a shining example—an order that bore the weight of moral imperative and altered the course of American history.

Throughout the 20th century, executive orders continued to be instrumental in catalyzing social transformation. The desegregation of the armed forces under Harry Truman and the establishment of internment camps for Japanese-Americans during World War II by Franklin D. Roosevelt are telltale signs of their wide-reaching implications. These executive directives, while rooted in a desire to swiftly address national concerns, paved complex legal and ethical pathways for future generations to navigate.

Each President has wielded executive orders with varying stead and strategy, prompting an ebb and flow in their use and the public's receptiveness. During the Roosevelt presidency, the sheer volume of orders issued was unparalleled, illustrating an era of rapid expansion of executive influence amid the exigencies of the Great Depression and a global war.

As the tapestry of the United States evolved, so too did the nature of executive orders. They became emblems of unilateral action, occasionally bypassing Congress when legislation stalled or fumbled at the feet of its own bureaucracy. They became, in essence, a lightning rod for constitutional debates, questioning the balance of power among the branches of government.

Sometimes, executive orders have promulgated policies that endured with little political pushback, such as the establishment of the Peace Corps by John F. Kennedy. In other instances, orders have provoked legal challenges and sweeping judicial decisions, testing the durability of checks and balances in practice.

The judicial system's oversight of executive actions ensures a measure of accountability, but does not always derail the momentum of a presidential decree. Such was the case with Truman's attempt to nationalize the steel mills during the Korean War, which was met with a firm rebuff by the Supreme Court, defining a boundary for executive authority. Yet, there remains an ongoing dialogue over the outer limits of executive command.

In more recent times, executive orders have been wielded amidst polarized political arenas, igniting passionate public discourse. They remain tools for swift action, often used in service of fulfilling campaign promises or redirecting national policy without the delay inherent in legislative processes.

However, one might ask, do these actions align with the spirit of the Constitution, the essence of democracy, and the notion of representative government? By circumventing the legislative branch, executive orders can be seen either as necessary responses to urgent matters or as overreaches that undermine the deliberative process.

Questions on the transparency and long-term effects of executive orders also rise to the forefront of constitutional consideration. The fine line between expedient governance and dictatorial titrations of power requires constant vigilance. The public's understanding of, and engagement with, this mechanism of executive authority is therefore paramount to maintaining a government that is both of the people and for the people.

It is in grasping the historical context and evolution of executive orders that one begins to appreciate their complexity and potency. They can be agents of liberation or control, progress or regression, reflecting the spectrum of presidential philosophies and the tides of public sentiment.

As guardians of liberty, there is a collective duty to scrutinize these executive directives, to question their intent and impact, and to ensure they do not stray from the core principles enshrined within our Constitution. This vigilance is not solely the responsibility of learned justices or legislators, but equally owed by every citizen, whose rights these orders affect directly or indirectly.

Upon reflection, the history of executive orders is a mirror reflecting the ever-changing profile of American governance. From its embryonic use by the nation's founders to the instrumental force it represents today, the story of executive orders is inseparable from the story of America's quest to balance the promise of swift action with the principle of collective assent.

Awareness and active participation in this aspect of governance are essential if the principles of the Constitution are to be honored and preserved. It's upon this understanding that we, the people, can truly harness the transformative power of our governance and direct it in a manner that resonates with the symphony of democracy and the ethos of the republic.

National Emergencies and Executive Authority
Understanding the scale and scope of a president's power
during times of national emergency is essential to grasp
the grander narrative of constitutional rights. The
National Emergencies Act of 1976 is a pivotal point,
granting presidents extensive authority to activate special
powers during a crisis. Yet, does this powerful tool align
with the Constitution? Careful scrutiny is demanded to
ensure that the invocation of emergency powers remains
a guardian of public welfare, not a backdoor to erode
fundamental liberties.

In the fabric of our Constitution, checks and balances
were meticulously woven to prevent the concentration of
power. The framers feared the consequences of
unchecked authority, perhaps foreseeing the potential
misuse of emergency powers as a threat to democratic
integrity. They sought to establish a system that protects
against the very human temptation to hold on to and
expand power in the face of crisis.

Presidential actions taken under the guise of emergencies
have historically stretched the boundaries of executive
authority. This trend raises a profound question: at what
point does the executive response to crisis become an
overreach? Analyzing historical instances of emergency
declarations, it's important to discern the line between
necessary action and opportunistic power grab.

When emergency powers are enacted, the ideological
landscape of our republic shifts. The balance tilts, and
executive discretion becomes the fulcrum. Laws can be
circumvented; liberties, once assumed unassailable, can
suddenly be compromised. Yet, it's essential to remember
that constitutional rights aren't granted by government;

they are inherent and must be fiercely defended, especially in challenging times. This reinforces the importance of vigorous legislative and judicial oversight, ensuring executive action is both effective and constitutionally sound.

Consider the role of public perception in such periods. A society under pressure may acquiesce to measures it might otherwise resist. This public sentiment can enable leaders to stretch the executive branch's reach, sometimes beyond what is reasonable or even lawful. Vigilance is required from both elected officials and citizens to prevent the erosion of civil liberties under the pretext of protection.

The invocation of a national emergency must never become a habitual tool for achieving political goals that fail to garner support through the standard legislative process. It's a dangerous precedent to set, for a true state of emergency to lose its significance and be invoked to circumvent Congressional authority or stifle dissent.

Emergencies have been used to justify extraordinary actions, such as the suspension of habeas corpus, internment of citizens, and the seizure of property. Each instance faced legal and ethical challenges, leading to debates that reverberate through history. Reviewing these cases, one can't help but wonder: have we learned from our past, or are we doomed to repeat it?

Central to this discussion is the concept of a "temporary" expansion of power. Often, what is introduced as a short-term necessity evolves into a permanent fixture. The rationale for these powers tends to persist, or be redefined, long after the initial crisis has abated. As such, sunset clauses and periodic reviews of emergency powers are vital safeguards, though they require staunch legislative backbone to ensure enforcement.

It cannot be overstated that the power to declare emergencies must not undermine the rule of law. Legal recourse must always be available to challenge executive decisions, maintaining the judiciary as a bulwark against potential abuses. The transparency of the decision-making process, public availability of evidence, and open debate are all necessary to maintain trust and prevent executive overreach.

In times of turmoil, leaders are tested, and the strength of constitutional principles are put to the proof. It's the shared responsibility of all branches of government—and indeed, of all citizens—to ensure that executive authority exercised in national emergencies strengthens, rather than undermines, the foundations of our freedom.

Conceptually, emergency powers are akin to a potent medicine that, while necessary to address a critical ailment, can become poison if dosed incorrectly or handled carelessly. Striking the delicate balance between effective crisis management and the preservation of civil liberties is a complex, but not insurmountable challenge.

The criterion for a national emergency must be specific, tangible, and justifiable. A state of emergency should be limited in duration and scope, always subject to scrutiny. It's pivotal that the process for declaring and reviewing a national emergency is transparent and accountable, providing the public insight into and control over the government's crisis response.

Moreover, unwavering focus must be maintained on preparedness and prevention. By investing in infrastructures of resilience, fostering innovation in public safety, and encouraging civic education, the need for emergency powers may be mitigated. Proactive measures lessen the potential for an emergency to serve as a gateway to overreach.

Reflecting upon our nation's history and the foresight of its founders, it's clear that they entrusted future generations with the obligation to uphold the constitutional framework—especially when that framework is under strain. We must not wane in our commitment to this duty; the safeguarding of liberties must be paramount, regardless of the challenges faced.

In conclusion, national emergencies and executive authority involve a dichotomy of protecting the nation while respecting the Constitution. As such, every American carries the responsibility to be informed, engaged, and resolute in defending our rights. For only through a collective commitment to our constitutional principles can we ensure that the response to one crisis does not precipitate another—in the form of compromised liberties and weakened rule of law.

The Unitary Executive Theory in Practice

As you turn the pages of this discourse, let's venture into a deep dive of a concept gaining traction within the walls of power. The Unitary Executive Theory is not just academic musing; it represents a profound shift in the balance of American governance. Envision a single, almost monarchial figure, wielding the entirety of executive power, unchecked by the usual balance of legislative and judicial counterweights. This is the essence of the Unitary Executive Theory.

At its core, the Unitary Executive Theory proposes that the President possesses the authority to control the entire executive branch. Historical precedents often provide glimpses of where ambitious leaders, armed with this theory, have flexed governmental muscles to overshadow the other branches.

Practically, this theory molds executive actions wherein presidential directives steamroll over established bureaucratic procedures. Often, the President's signature is the final word, de facto rendering the advice and consent of other bodies moot.

The War Powers Resolution is one such battleground for this theory. Executives have tested, bent, and sometimes bypassed congressionally mandated checks on their authority to wage war, a domain constitutionally shared with the legislature.

Executive Orders are the paintbrushes of this unitary paradigm. Their use, historically varied and cautious, has become more decisive, with Presidents issuing edicts that reshape domestic and foreign policies, tiptoeing on the edge of legislative territory.

Consider the Federal agencies, whose leaders serve at the pleasure of the President. Here, under the unitary vision, appointees push presidential agendas forward, often circumventing the collaborative regulatory process expected in a more balanced approach.

National Emergencies have granted fertile ground for Presidents to exercise unilateral power. Under the guise of crisis management, executive discretion widens, bending the arc of governance towards a singular apex of command and control.

Immigration policy offers an illustrative case study. The discretion granted to the executive often translates into sweeping reforms and enforcement directives, which alter the fabric of communities and the economy, without going through the crucible of congressional debate and public scrutiny.

The judiciary, meant as a check, grapples with the swift currents of the executive's actions. They can challenge or uphold presidential prerogatives, but such processes are frequently slowed by the courts' inherent deliberative pace, often allowing executive decisions to take root before judgment is passed.

The implications for civil liberties are immediate and personal. Under the thrust of unitary power, privacy concerns arise as surveillance mechanisms multiply, often masquerading as vital national interests, with the individual's voice marginalized in its wake.

Due process, a cornerstone of justice, can erode under the weight of a unitary executive, as agencies become the judge, jury, and sometimes executioner, of their mandates, diluting the possibility of fair recourse for the individual.

Whistleblowers find themselves in the crosshairs, targeted by administrations that view dissent through the lens of protecting homogenized executive ambition rather than as a healthy part of democratic checks and balances.

Transparency takes a backseat as the executive branch centralizes control. Under such concentrated authority, information flows are managed to serve the narrative of executive efficiency, often at the expense of candor and accountability.

Congressional oversight, the people's watchdog, strains under the Unitary Executive Theory. Legislators find themselves on a backfoot, confronting a consolidated executive that announces decisions more often than it consults or cooperates with the legislature.

The tide of the Unitary Executive Theory ebbs and flows with the whims of each Presidential administration. Yet, the precedents it sets linger, incrementally reshaping the governance landscape. It underscores the imperativeness for vigilance, for informed citizenry, and for steadfast defense of the Constitution, which enshrines not the might of one but the power of many, in service of all.

Chapter 13: Legislative Loopholes: Lawmaking or Liberty Taking?

The potency of our nation's foundations is tested when the art of lawmaking morphs subtly into an exercise of liberty taking. This chapter uncovers the veiled dynamics at play in our legislative chambers, where the power of the purse strings tightens around the core of democracy, and bureaucratic reach often extends beyond its rightful grasp. These loopholes, concealed within the mundane prose of legal texts, carry the weight to erode our representation in the very halls designed to champion it. We examine closely how regulatory powers, through the passage of obscure and convoluted laws, swiftly encroach upon individual freedoms, leaving citizens to grapple with the ramifications of decisions made in their name but without their clear consent. The call to action is now; remaining vigilant is not a passive stance but rather a conscious, unyielding commitment to safeguarding our liberties from those who subtly, but steadily, aim to redefine the boundaries of authority.

The Power of the Purse Strings - In the intricate dance of checks and balances outlined by the U.S. Constitution, the legislative branch was endowed with a pivotal tool: the power to control federal spending. This authority, often less glory-laden than executive orders or judicial review, carries within it the profound potential to shape the nation's course.

Consider the basic civics behind this power: Congress, the people's representatives, controls the budget. This singular power, to fund or to withhold funds, impacts everything from military operations to social programs. The allocation of resources is not merely an act of balancing ledgers; it speaks to the very priorities of a nation and the rights of the people.

Yet, here, amid the rising crescendos of political discourse, lies a subtle but invasive threat to constitutional rights. When control of the budget becomes a political weapon rather than a tool for governance, it can undermine the foundational principles of democracy.

It is crucial to dissect how and why this weaponization occurs. For instance, the withholding of funds for certain programs can become an indirect method of dismantling legislation without the due process of law—effectively eroding the legislative process. Similarly, the misdirection of funds counter to the expressed intent of Congress can dilute the effectiveness of the checks and balances system.

The potency of the power of the purse is evident in its historical employment. Take, for example, how budgetary constraints have been used to limit actions of the executive branch. By tightening or loosening the financial reins, Congress can significantly hamper or enable presidential initiatives.

However, the strength of the budgetary power can also be turned inwards. It's used to affect judicial outcomes by funding, or defunding, certain programs within the Department of Justice or influencing the execution of laws by adjusting the budgets of enforcing agencies. Such fiscal maneuvers can sway the perceived impartiality of the justice system and erode public trust in its efficacy.

Moreover, citizen rights can be directly influenced by financial decisions made far from public eyes. Consider how priorities established in secret budget sessions can lead to increased surveillance, a threat to privacy all too real in our digital age, without proper public discourse or challenge. This isn't just theory; it's an existing concern that requires constant vigilance.

The captious nature of budgetary control extends also to its role in social policy. Funding allocations impact the quality and availability of education, healthcare, and social services, drawing lines that define societal equity and opportunity. Budgets effectively shape the landscape of who gets what, when, and how in America.

There's no denying the tension that this power produces. Fiscal decisions can be seen as the deliberative pulse of the legislative body, a reflection of the values and visions of those elected to represent the public. The battlefield of budgetary control is fought not solely on the floors of Congress but in the day-to-day lives of citizens.

Power of the purse is not simply about money; it's about manifesting ideals into tangible reality. When properly wielded, it safeguards liberties and promotes the general welfare. Misused, it stifles freedoms and props up unjust systems. It is an indicator of our times, a symbol of the political will, and, most potently, a litmus test for the health of our democracy.

Citizens must engage with this process, must understand the nuances of budgetary debates, and see beyond partisan rhetoric to the implications for rights and liberties. Ignorance here is not bliss; it is acquiescence to the erosion of the very fabric of our freedoms.

Fiscal scrutiny is not solely the domain of economists and policy wonks; it is the prerogative of every citizen who values the rights and liberties promised by the Constitution. The power of the purse, while abstract, deals in the currency of real lives—the funding for a child's education, the resources for a family's health, the security of a nation's freedoms.

To conclude, let's affirm that speaking up, staying informed, and holding representatives accountable for fiscal decisions are paramount. The intricacies of budgets might seem daunting, but they are decipherable, impactful, and directly related to our rights. Embrace the challenge to understand. Advocate for transparency and accountability. And recognize that financial decisions are, in essence, moral declarations of who we are and aspire to be as a nation.

The persuasive charge, then, for all engaged citizens, is to monitor the wielders of the purse strings closely. Democracy thrives on active participation, and nothing is more critical to its sustenance than the informed oversight of its fiscal policies. In the words that grace our nation's founding document, to "secure the blessings of liberty to ourselves and our posterity" requires more than passive hope—it demands vigilant, informed, and active stewardship of our constitutional rights.

Regulating Beyond Reach Within the complex web of liberty and law, there exists an ambitious arm of governance: regulation. Regulation, in its essence, can serve the public good, setting standards for health, safety, and welfare. Yet, when it extends beyond its intended reach, it enters a sphere where the authority to regulate can clash with constitutional rights.

The power to regulate must not become a blank check for encroachment on liberties. When laws morph into tools of convenience for those governing rather than instruments safeguarding the governed, a fundamental shift occurs—an overreach, very subtle yet profound in its consequences.

Consider the illustration of a frog in tepid water, with the heat increasing incrementally. The frog fails to jump out because the change is gradual, and it does not perceive the danger until it's too late. Similarly, excessive regulations often expand over time, slowly encroaching upon our rights, making it harder for individuals to realize the true extent of their loss until much of their freedoms have been eroded. This phenomenon isn't hypothetical—it's a tangible shift that has historical precedent and presents-day ramifications.

Overregulation can manifest in various domains, such as the workplace, the environment, and even personal lifestyle choices. From immense codes dictating the minutiae of business operations, to intricate rules guiding environmental actions, down to the restrictions on personal habits, these regulations, pieced together, form a tapestry of control, subtle in its stitching but capable of entangling the very people it's meant to protect.

Moreover, in this modern era, technology has opened doors to regulatory power that the framers of the Constitution could not have envisioned. With every byte and bit of data collected, there's potential for misuse in the guise of regulation. Consider how surveillance under the mantle of public safety can lead to infringements on privacy, a right held dear under the Constitution.

Examining this regulatory reach also requires a recognition of the shift in balance between the three branches of government. Congress, with its legislative authority, has at times abdicated its responsibility to detailed legislating, deferring instead to executive agencies that then promulgate regulations with little oversight. This process not only sidesteps the rigorous debate and compromise that should accompany any curtailment of liberties but also circumvents the checks and balances designed to prevent any one branch from wielding unchecked power.

Another dimension of regulatory overreach is in its potential favoritism and uneven application. When complex regulations favor large corporations with the resources to navigate and even influence the regulatory landscape, small businesses and individuals are left at a disadvantage. This imbalance in implementation can create an unequal playing field, contrary to the constitutional ethos of equal protection and opportunity.

So profound is the impact of regulatory incursions that even the most fundamental aspects of life, like property ownership, can become mired in layers of regulatory approvals. The process to build a home, to start a business, or even to speak publicly can become so convoluted with regulatory hurdles that the notions of property rights and free speech are compromised.

Tackling this system of overreach calls for citizens to not only understand their rights but to actively engage in the processes that govern them. It entails a vigilance to hold lawmakers and enforcers accountable, ensuring that regulations serve the public and do not subvert the foundational principles of freedom.

The recalibration of this balance requires a renaissance of civic participation. It seeks a populace informed and impassioned enough to champion the cause of liberty. It demands discourse, transparency, and above all, a collective will to uphold the tenets of the Constitution.

As regulations continue to outpace the ability of an average person to keep track, it challenges us to consider the trajectory of governance. Are we advancing toward an era of unwarranted control, or can we redirect the course to preserve the liberties that define us?

Indeed, therein lies the charge for each citizen: to not be passive spectators but active participants in the shaping of regulatory frameworks. To engage with lawmakers, attend public hearings, and create dialogues that bring about regulations which reflect the spirit of the Constitution rather than undermine it.

Looking ahead, the responsibility to constrain regulatory overreach does not solely rest on the shoulders of the government but also on the citizenry. It is through collective efforts that the delicate balance between effective regulation and the preservation of rights is maintained, ensuring that the reach of regulation does not extend beyond the constitutional grip.

As this dialogue continues, let us remember that the Constitution was penned not just as a document of governance but as a charter of liberties. It speaks not of the power to regulate but of the power to protect— protect the rights, the freedoms, and the inherent dignity of every individual against the convenience of unbounded regulation.

In essence, the strength of a constitutionally-guided democracy lies in its respect for the line between lawful governance and liberty infringement. Vigilance against regulatory overreach is not merely a legal necessity but a manifestation of our deepest commitment to the values of America's founding. This is a call for awareness, courage, and action. It is time to reassess and reclaim the freedoms intended for us, ensuring that the reach of regulation remains firmly within the bounds of our constitutional rights.

Erosion of Representation - it's a phrase that may not stir the soul at first mention, yet it's at the heart of today's battle for the preservation of our Constitutional rights. The notion that individuals are becoming increasingly powerless in impacting the legislative decisions that shape their lives is not just alarming—it strikes at the core of the democratic process. So let's unpack this quietly pervasive issue and its rippling effects on the hallowed halls of Congress and the town squares of America.

Representation is the bedrock of American governance. The architects of the Constitution designed a system where the people, through their chosen representatives, wield the power. Yet, as time marches on, this fundamental principle is being eroded by forces both seen and unseen. The question isn't merely if this is happening, but rather what mechanisms are at play and how deeply they've undermined the republic's foundation.

Consider the mundane but mighty force of gerrymandering—the redrawing of electoral districts. It's an art as old as the republic itself, often used to consolidate power rather than reflect the will of the people. Districts are engineered to create safe seats, resulting in legislators who are more responsive to the dictates of their party than to the diverse voices of their constituents. Thus, a great disconnect grows, and the notion of true representation withers on the vine.

Compounding this is the avalanche of money that buries the democratic process. When campaign coffers outweigh the collective voice, when legislators must bow to the might of financial benefactors, who then are they truly representing? The advent of super PACs and the ripple effects of cases like Citizens United have turned the political arena into an arms race of dollars and donations, distancing the average citizen from the levers of power.

Frustration brews among voters, who sense their diminishing power. Voter turnout statistics are a sobering reflection of this disillusionment. Moreover, disenfranchisement isn't just about apathy—it's often about systemic barriers. Voter ID laws, purges of voter rolls, and the curtailing of early voting and absentee ballots contribute to the depreciation of the individual's say in the electoral forum.

The functional obsolescence of political parties is another factor in the erosion of representation. These entities, which should be instruments for the aggregation of beliefs and policy preferences, have become sclerotic, often more concerned with maintaining power than with responding to the evolving priorities and needs of their members.

Lobbying, in principle, is a legitimate part of the democratic process, allowing individuals and organizations to advocate for their interests. In practice, however, it has morphed into a Goliath overshadowing the democratic David. The influence industry not only peddles in dollars but in the crafting of legislation itself, often penning the very bills that become the laws of the land, sidelining the citizenry in the process.

All these forces coalesce into an unsettling picture where representation is not just eroded but gutted, leaving a hull where once there was a powerful vessel of participatory democracy. It paints a legislature not of people's servants, but of figures ensconced in a citadel of self-interest and external influence.

Yet, within this gloomy diagnosis, there lies the potential for powerful remedies. Awareness can breed action, and collective resolve can reset the system. It starts with recognizing the power of voting—not merely as an act of civic duty, but as an assertion of rights and a reaffirmation of the power vested in the individual. Each vote is a building block in the reconstruction of a representative edifice.

Reforming the redistricting process to eliminate gerrymandering holds the promise of creating a more equitable and true reflection of the populace. Independent commissions, rather than partisan legislatures, should be tasked with drawing district lines, ensuring that communities are represented by those who truly reflect their makeup and concerns.

Similarly, campaign finance reform is paramount. The call for transparency in funding and capping contributions isn't radical; it's a return to the essence of representation. Movements to overturn Supreme Court decisions that equate money with speech must continue to gain steam, voicing the creed that democracy should not be auctioned to the highest bidder.

Voting rights must be fiercely protected. The eradication of policies that disenfranchise must be pursued relentlessly, ensuring that every citizen has unimpeded access to the ballot box. From automatic voter registration to the restoration of voting rights for disenfranchised populations, we can reimagine a more inclusive electorate.

The revitalization of political parties will demand grassroots energy—a return to local issues and constituencies, where the civic fabric is woven strongest. Empowering the local level can dilute the concentration of power and create a more responsive and dynamic party system that mirrors the changing contours of the American populace.

The lobbying machine must be reined in. By instituting robust lobbying reforms and ensuring greater transparency, the invisible hand that often guides legislation can be made visible and made to serve, rather than circumvent, the interests of the public.

In the erosion of representation lies the seed of rejuvenation. Citizens must reclaim their rightful place in the halls of governance. Let this call to action not be a whisper in the wind but a rallying cry that reverberates in the chambers of power and the streets of every town. It is not just our right, but our solemn duty, to restore the equilibrium of power—to ensure that government remains, by the people and for the people, henceforth and forever.

Chapter 14: The Eleventh Through Twenty-Seventh Amendments: Contemporary Context

Embark on a journey through the less traversed paths of the Eleventh through Twenty-Seventh Amendments, where the tenets of our justice and democratic systems are both fortified and challenged. In an era where each news cycle triggers a fresh bout of constitutional debate, these amendments provide a framework that, while essential, is often overshadowed by the more frequently cited Bill of Rights. From remolding how senators are elected to ensuring that no president serves a dictatorial term, these amendments have shaped the American political and social landscape in ways that demand vigilant guardianship. As we navigate through these modern times, the relevance of these amendments cannot be understated—they are pillars that support fundamental changes while being, far too often, used as pawns in the grand chess game of political gambits. This chapter dissects the dynamic interplay between historical intention and present deviation, reminding us that our constitutional fabric is only as strong as our collective commitment to preserving its integrity. Seize this knowledge and become empowered to advocate for a future that truly reflects the visionary essence of constitutional rights and balances.

Strengthening and Subverting the Structural Amendments The fabric of a nation's constitution isn't immune to the call of time and change. Amending the foundational document is a testament to our society's evolution and to the foresight of the Framers. But as we delve into the eleven through twenty-seventh amendments, we encounter a spectrum where such alterations have both fortified and potentially undermined the very structure they were meant to safeguard. It's not merely about the addition of words on parchment; it's a matter of how those words have been interpreted and, sometimes, reinterpreted to the point where their original purpose is all but unrecognizable.

A robust democracy thrives on informed debate and the dynamic interplay between the people's will and constitutional integrity. The amendments have been a battleground where, for better or worse, some of the most critical fights for liberty, equality, and justice have taken place. They're the pressure points of our constitution, areas where the slightest push can send shockwaves through the system, bringing both progress and challenges.

Take for example, the Fourteenth Amendment. Initially created to ensure the rights of freed slaves, it has since become a critical tool in the fight for civil rights for all Americans. It's a powerful example of an amendment that has fortified the pillars of American society by broadening the scope of liberty and equality. Yet it has also been used in ways that perhaps its drafters never envisioned, adding nuance to constitutional discourse through interpretations of due process and equal protection.

Conversely, the interpretation of the Eleventh Amendment has sometimes served to subvert the initial intention of granting individuals redress against states. Over time, the Supreme Court's interpretation has often strengthened state sovereignty at the expense of individuals' ability to seek justice, illustrating how an amendment can be perceived as both strengthening and diminishing the architecture of constitutional rights.

The Seventeenth Amendment, providing for the direct election of senators, championed democracy by giving voice to the people, a strengthening move shifting power away from state legislatures and into the hands of the electorate. It sought to curb corruption and ensure that senators would be more responsive to public concerns. Yet, some argue it has also distanced senators from state issues, focusing their attention more on national agendas and the desires of political parties, hence subverting the regional balance intended by the Framers.

When we come to the Nineteenth Amendment, securing women the right to vote, we see a colossal leap forward for democratic principles. This single change tore down centuries-old barriers and invigorated the Constitution with a fresh spirit of inclusiveness. However, even after its ratification, systemic subversion persisted through discriminations that kept countless citizens from the polls, reflecting a gap between the amendment's letter and spirit.

The evolution of the Second Amendment is a striking case of contention, with current events bringing its interpretation into heated debate. Once considered a safeguard for a citizen's right to self-defense and resistance to tyranny, its modern-day application has unveiled rifts in public sentiment, sparking discussions about the balance between individual rights and collective safety.

The Twenty-Second Amendment, limiting presidential terms, was a structural reinforcement to avoid the possibility of a leader for life, which could threaten the very foundations of a republican form of government. Yet, by cementing this rule into the fabric of the Constitution, it has also been argued that it limits the democratic choice of the people, assuming they wish to elect a leader consecutively.

The Twenty-sixth Amendment, lowering the voting age to eighteen, was another affirmation of democratic values, recognizing the maturity and voice of America's youth. While it unquestionably strengthened the electorate, skeptics might point out it has not been without its subversions, considering the consistently low voter turnout among the young population, which suggests a disconnect between the extension of a right and its robust exercise.

Amid these examples lie countless other minutiae, where each amendment carries a dual-edged sword: the possibility of supporting the edifice of democracy while occasionally chipping away at its columns. These consequences aren't preordained; they are the result of human action and judicial interpretation. The lesson? Our engagement with these amendments can't be passive. We must be vigilant architects, always working to ensure that these structural changes stand solidly upon the intent to extend and protect liberties, not confine them.

We're at a crucial juncture where understanding is more than power—it's a responsibility. It falls upon each of us to scrutinize how these amendments function in practice, how they affect our lives daily, and how they can be both - a shield to guard our liberties and sometimes a tool that digs at their very roots.

This scrutiny isn't a task reserved for legal experts; it's a duty for every citizen with a stake in the society they inhabit. It's about peeling back the layers to see what's working and what isn't, what's upholding the Constitution's promises, and what's undermining them. Standing on the sidelines while these amendments are interpreted and reinterpreted without our input gives room for liberties to be whittled away—often without us even noticing.

The structural amendments, spanning issues from who can vote to the balance of power between federal and state governments, all hinge on a public that's both mindful and discerning. Our democracy is only as strong as the engagement of its citizens with these critical touchstones of our constitutional system. Passive citizens allow subtle subversions; active citizens foster the strengthening of their government by the rule of the people, for the people, and by the people.

In the end, the true strength of the structural amendments lies not in their wording alone but in the spirit with which they are embraced and the vigilance with which they are protected. It's about acknowledging the fluid nature of our living Constitution—the way it adapts, grows, and, yes, sometimes, veers off course. This acknowledgment is the first step in either shoring up the structure or, when necessary, steering it back to its original path of justice, liberty, and equality for all.

Remaining Amendments: Relevance and Reality

The American Constitution stands as a beacon of hope—a testament to freedom and a framework for the rule of law. Yet, the amendments beyond the cherished first ten, known as the Bill of Rights, are often overshadowed. They are fundamental components defining our republic, from the nuances of legal processes to the limits of power. Understanding each amendment in contemporary context not only educates but also empowers citizens to recognize when these principles are manipulated or ignored.

The Eleventh Amendment established sovereign immunity, clarifying judicial boundaries to states' susceptibility to suits from out-of-state citizens. Today, this amendment remains a bulwark against federal overreach, yet few citizens grasp its pertinence. Instances of governmental entities overstepping their bounds urge us to revisit the foundation that guards states' rights against overwhelming centralized power.

Then there is the Twelfth Amendment, reshaping the electoral process for the president and vice president, ensuring that these offices reflect the people's choice more accurately. Its complexities come to life during every election cycle, significantly influencing the balance between the popular vote and the Electoral College—a subject regularly sparking debates on its modern-day application.

Diving into the civil war amendments—thirteenth, fourteenth, and fifteenth—these monumental changes to the Constitution eradicated slavery, assured equal protection under the law, and protected voting rights regardless of race. However, their invoking in contemporary issues, such as debates on affirmative action, voting ID laws, and the struggle against systemic racism, illustrates that the battle for their complete fruition continues.

The Sixteenth Amendment, authorizing the federal income tax, profoundly impacts every wage-earning American. Still, questions arise about its reach and the burgeoning complexity of the tax code. Herein lies an intersection of law and the individual's financial liberty, where public understanding could cultivate more informed debates on governmental fiscal policy.

The Senatorial elections, once the purview of state legislatures, were democratized through the Seventeenth Amendment. Yet, it begs reflection whether this shift has brought the Senate closer to the citizenry or if it has inadvertently distanced common concerns from Congressional halls.

The Eighteenth Amendment's introduction of prohibition, later repealed by the Twenty-First, serves as a stark reminder of how constitutional changes can affect American social fabric. This historical lesson prompts us to consider whether certain amendments have, in their essence, overstepped their marks on regulating morality.

Women's suffrage, marked by the Nineteenth Amendment, significantly shaped American democracy. Its relevance remains unquestioned, as it's a daily reality for half the population whose political voice was once silenced. Nonetheless, the struggle for equal rights and equal pay indicates the continued journey toward the amendment's complete actualization.

Subsequent amendments, such as the Twenty-Second, which limits presidential terms, and the Twenty-Fifth, delineating presidential succession, are crucial to maintaining balance in the executive branch. These set tangible limits on power, fostering a political climate where no single individual can dictate beyond a defined scope—urgent frameworks in an era where executive overreach is a pressing concern.

The Twenty-Sixth Amendment, lowering the voting age to eighteen, encapsulates an ever-renewing faith in the youth of America. By granting them the vote, it acknowledges their stake in the nation's future. Yet, as voter engagement among the youth wavers, the impetus falls on society to ignite the political fervor that this amendment embodies.

Finally, the Twenty-Seventh Amendment, addressing congressional pay adjustments, arguably one of the lesser-discussed amendments, holds legislators accountable to the electorate. Its late ratification, almost two centuries after proposal, suggests a constitutional resilience, reminding us that change is possible, albeit slow, often at the pace of collective will.

Each amendment beyond the Bill of Rights carries with it stories of America's growth, challenges, and redefinitions of liberty. Engagement with these tenets should not merely be academic but a part of everyday consciousness. For when legislative, executive, or judicial action veers into the territory of eroding rights, awareness and understanding of these amendments provide the first line of defense.

Moreover, the reality that these amendments face today is that they are not merely historical footnotes but living instruments that impact daily American life. To acknowledge their significance is to understand the immense power inherently held within an informed populace. For it is not just the responsibility of the courts or elected officials to uphold these amendments but every citizen's duty to ensure their proper application and respect.

A clear grasp of these amendments illuminates the path to a fuller democracy and more perfect union that the Constitution envisions. Embracing the relevance and appreciating the reality of these amendments serves as a solid foundation for civic engagement—where citizens are truly the custodians of their own liberties, and through them, the guardians of the Constitution.

Therefore, let us embrace the collective journey into the heart of what these amendments stand for, appreciate their place in the contemporary world, and commit to the vigilant protection of the rights they guarantee. Therein lies the true strength of a free society—a society vigilant in the face of apathy, persuasive in its quest for justice, and forever aspiring to the ideals etched within its founding document. Thus, the relevance and reality of these remaining amendments cannot be overstated; they are the tapestry of our nation's constitutional commitments, evolving yet enduring, awaiting our unwavering support and dedication.

Chapter 15: Citizens Arise: Restoring Constitutional Governance

In the shadow of creeping overreach and the subtle dimming of constitutional lights, a new dawn beckons with the clarion call for civic action. As this chapter unfolds, so too does the roadmap for reclaiming the very essence of our republic. It isn't about casting blame or lingering in despair over the missteps that have led us here; it's about the collective stride towards an educated, unified, and vigilant populace that holds the torch of freedom high and unwavering. This narrative equips you with the quintessential truths of our founding principles and provides the crucial pivot from passive observer to active participant in our democracy. It's within the grasp of each citizen—from the fervent whispers of grassroots movements to the echoed chants in the halls of justice—to ignite the flame of liberty once more. Let this chapter serve not as a finale, but a beginning, where every American becomes a custodian of justice, ensuring that our constitutional governance isn't merely restored, but revitalized for generations to come.

Knowledge is Power: Educating the Populace

Knowledge truly is power, and nowhere is this truer than in the struggle to protect our constitutional rights. Ignorance is not just a simple lack of information; it's a chain that keeps citizens shackled, preventing them from recognizing and challenging the violations of their freedoms. In this quest for a restored constitutional governance, the first step is to educate ourselves and those around us.

The framers of the Constitution gifted us with more than just a set of laws; they provided a blueprint for participation in our democracy. Understanding this blueprint is critical. It's time to seize this knowledge and harness its power.

Look, liberties aren't eroded overnight. It happens gradually, subtly, and often under the guise of necessity. Recall the debates we've had surrounding national security and the trade-offs with personal privacy. Every piece of legislation, every executive order, every judicial interpretation either upholds the Constitution or chips away at its foundation. But too often, we've been unaware of the stakes.

So, what's the game plan? Dive headfirst into the core documents that define our nation - the Constitution, the Federalist Papers, landmark Supreme Court decisions. They're not just historical artifacts; they're living instruments that guide us in contemporary society. When we understand these documents, we become formidable guardians of our own rights.

Moreover, let's recognize that education doesn't stop at what's been written long ago. Staying informed about current events, government actions, and legislative changes is part of our civic duty. Recognizing patterns of overreach requires a well-informed populace that's up-to-date and alert.

It's essential to remember that knowledge without application is wasted potential. We must put what we learn into action. This starts with talking to our neighbors, engaging in community forums, and participating in local government.

Facilitating access to this information equates to empowering each citizen. Let's burst the bubbles created by misinformation and polarized media landscapes. Tools for critical thinking and resources for independent verification should be as widely distributed as the air we breathe.

Public libraries, schools, and community centers should evolve into hubs of civic education. Workshops on constitutional rights, debates on policy implications, and seminars on civil liberties could be as common as sporting events.

In these pursuits, the use of technology can be a double-edged sword. While it has the potential to mislead with misinformation, it also has unparalleled ability to educate and mobilize. Online platforms can host a wealth of resources ranging from interactive constitutions to databases of politicians' voting records. Let these tools serve the cause of education.

A crucial aspect in fostering an educated populace is to encourage critical thinking rather than passive consumption of information. Each citizen should be equipped to ask the right questions, seek out multiple perspectives, and challenge the narratives presented to them.

And let's not overlook the need to inspire the next generation. Educational curricula should reinforce the importance of the Constitution and the role it plays in everyday life. Youth should emerge from education systems not only as job-ready but as democracy-ready citizens.

Some may fear the consequences of a population skilled in the art of critical thought, but it is precisely these individuals who will lead the charge in restoring constitutional governance. They will become the lawmakers, judges, and leaders who respect the constraints of the Constitution.

We must also embrace the role of non-traditional education. Podcasts, social media campaigns, and even art can convey powerful messages about civil liberties. The goal is to permeate society with an understanding of and appreciation for constitutional rights.

Mobilizing minds is the precursor to mobilizing action. With a populace that values its rights and knows how to defend them, no politician, no judge, no president can easily undermine the cornerstones of our freedom.

It all starts with knowledge, with education. The more we know, the stronger we stand. So, let's commit ourselves to becoming constitutional connoisseurs—safeguarding liberty and justice as our way of life, not just as concepts in parchment under glass. This is how we lay the foundation for a future where constitutional governance isn't just an ideal, but a reality. This is how we claim the power that has always been rightfully ours.

Grassroots Movements and Their Impact often begin as a flicker of defiance, a spark of belief in justice and equality that burns against the tide of apathy. They are a testament to the power of the collective when individuals, empowered by their convictions, unite for a cause. Yet, the true measure of their significance lies not just in their beginnings but in their ability to transform landscapes—political, social, and judicial—especially when constitutional rights feel besieged.

In the fabrics of history, we find these movements tightly woven. From the suffragettes fighting for women's rights to the civil rights advocates marching for equality, grassroots initiatives have always been at the forefront of change. These movements gain their strength from their base—the ordinary citizens who often feel the sting of governmental overreach and constitutional neglect the most acutely.

Yet, grappling with the notion of initiating change can be daunting, can't it? It demands commitment, perseverance, and, above all, a belief that change is possible. It's about harnessing the power of the collective voice to safeguard the liberties enshrined in the Constitution that, all too often, are encroached upon by the very institutions meant to protect them.

Consider the Patriot Act, a controversial piece of legislature that stands as a testament to government overreach. Grassroots movements have tirelessly worked to educate the public about its implications on privacy—a Fourth Amendment right. The ripples of their efforts are unmistakable in the push for reforms and the heightened awareness around such issues.

It is through grassroots activism that awareness is raised and communities mobilized. Effective movements have the power to shine a light on obscure laws and executive actions that may violate constitutional rights, compelling citizens to question and challenge them. This is where change begins—with the awakening of consciousness in each individual.

The beauty of grassroots movements lies in their diversity and adaptability. They can start in a neighborhood meeting, on college campuses, or take shape online, transcending physical boundaries. This flexibility allows them to advocate for a broad range of issues—whether it be for free speech, against unwarranted search and seizure, or gun rights as ensured by the Second Amendment.

Movement building, at its core, is about cultivating solidarity. When individuals realize they're not alone in their concerns, a community forms—a community that's focused on restoring governance that respects constitutional guarantees. It's an exertion of democracy in its purest form, where the governing powers are reminded that they derive their power from the consent of the governed.

It's not always a dramatic overthrow of policies or a sweeping legislative reform that marks the success of grassroots efforts. Success can also be incremental, seen in the small yet persistent steps that lead to greater accountability and transparency in governance. It is the tireless work of activists that often paves the way for court rulings that reinforce constitutional protections.

Yet, it's essential to confront the complexities of these movements. Not all have the same resources or reach; some voices are drowned out by louder, more dominant narratives. This is why inclusivity is crucial. A movement that represents the true spectrum of the community's beliefs and experiences is more enduring and impactful.

Moreover, victories for grassroots organizations are not just in the legal or policy changes they help usher in. The cultural impact—how they change conversations in living rooms, on social media, and in the media—is just as significant. They redefine the terms of debate, bringing constitutional rights back into focus, making them personal and relevant to individuals' daily lives.

In recent times, issues like net neutrality, police accountability, and environmental justice have witnessed a surge in grassroots activism. Each cause, in its way, connects to the tenets of the Constitution—from First Amendment rights to protection against unreasonable government intrusion.

Activists in these movements are not just fighting against something; they're also advocating for a vision of society that aligns with constitutional values. It's an active pursuit of a nation where governance is not just by the people, but for the people, in every sense of the phrase.

Change is never easy, nor is it immediate, but the impact of grassroots movements in influencing society and policy cannot be understated. By promoting civic education and engagement, these movements empower citizens to hold their government accountable and to ensure that their constitutional rights are more than just written words—they are living, breathing promises to every American.

As movements grow and evolve, they inspire the next generation of activists and concerned citizens. Through their dedication, they demonstrate that vast oceans are crossed drop by drop, and that even the seemingly insurmountable edifices of government overreach can be eroded through the steady drip of an engaged and vigilant populace.

The story of grassroots movements is ongoing—one of challenges, triumphs, and resilience. It's a story that invites each citizen to be an active participant, to contribute their voice, their time, and their passion. For when united, the people become a formidable force—one that can shape the destiny of a nation and ensure the enduring vitality of its constitutional foundations.

Civic Engagement: The Path to Change

Empowerment germinates from the seed of knowledge. In the quest for restoring Constitutional governance, engagement rings as the requisite clarion call that echoes the need for action. It's a sentiment that stirs the spirit, calling for individuals to step out of complacency's shadow and into the arena of change. The essence, the very heartbeat of democracy, lies in the active participation of its citizens. Civic engagement embeds itself as the bridge spanning the chasm between the present state of affairs and the ideal manifestation of rights as enshrined within the Constitution.

It is vital to recognize that apathy serves as the greatest ally to overreach—when the vigilant eye of the citizen dims, the reach of governance tends to extend unchecked. The transformation from passive observers to proactive participants isn't a leap but rather a series of intentional, informed steps. It's these steps that ignite the transformational journey of civic engagement—a journey that reintroduces the power of the aggregated voice.

The journey begins with a fundamental understanding of one's rights. This foundational step weaves through the fabric of the community, emboldening each thread to withstand the pressures of unconstitutional measures. As individuals grow in knowledge, accessing resources for further study becomes more than a character in a book or a footnote on a page; It becomes a weapon sharpened for defense and offense against liberty's erosions.

But knowledge alone does not suffice. It must translate into actionable strategies that target the cracks in the edifice of justice and governance. It is here, in the realm of action, where strategy meets street—town halls, school boards, community meetings. These are the platforms upon which voices unite, and the wisdom of accumulated knowledge gets amplified into a resonant chorus for change.

Grassroots movements have historically painted the horizon with the colors of transformation. The power of localized, bottom-up approaches to activism is immense. Without the burden of cumbersome bureaucracies, movements find the flexibility to adapt rapidly to dynamic political landscapes and direct resources where they're most urgently needed. A grassroots approach isn't limited to mass movements; it's an anthem that can be sung by any individual crusading for the nation's constitutional integrity.

Engagement isn't a solitary endeavor; collaboration breeds strength. Coalitions and alliances across the spectrum of viewpoints stand as testament to the adage that there is strength in numbers. It is through the pooling of resources, networks, and influence that small ripples magnify into formidable waves capable of eroding pillars of oppression and overreach.

Voting is perhaps the most recognized form of civic participation, and yet its significance is often diminished in the collective psyche. Each ballot cast is a testament to a citizen's presence, a declaration of intent, and a brick in the safeguarding wall around Constitutional rights. Elections at every tier of governance matter, for the local dais can be as impactful as the national stage.

Engagement extends to vigilant oversight of enforcement and implementation. Advocacy doesn't draw its final breath at the closing of the voting booth curtain. Instead, it persists, scrutinizing the actions of the elected and holding them accountable to the Constitutional benchmarks set forth by the founders and refined by the evolution of a conscious society.

Litigation, as a tool, holds a prominent place on the chessboard of change. The judicial branch presents an arduous yet essential battleground for correcting constitutional waywardness. Legal challenges require not only familiarity with the intricacies of the Constitution but also an unwavering resolve to contest violations irrespective of the adversary's stature.

Persistent inclusivity invites new perspectives and ideas into the fold. Change is not served by unanimity but rather fortified by the kaleidoscope of diversity. Engagement hails the joining of disparate voices in a concerted mission to reshape the narrative—a narrative currently knit by threads at odds with the constitutional loom.

Media, both traditional and new, offer avenues of self-expression and rallying cries for gathering. Harnessing the power of the pen and the screen, citizens can illuminate the darkened corners where constitutional breaches lay hidden, beckoning the collective gaze to witness and to respond. The narrative constructed within the public domain plays a pivotal role in shaping perceptions and influencing the trajectory of activism.

Education as activism presents itself as another vital stream. By fostering a culture of constitutional literacy starting from classrooms to community centers, individuals inoculate future generations against the recurrence of erosions. A society versed in the language of its rights is better prepared to contribute constructively to the discourse and practice of civics.

Patience, paired with persistent effort, is the often understated virtue of engagement. Change rarely occurs overnight; it is engineered through sustained pressure and the incremental accumulation of victories, small and large. This tireless vigilance manifests the resilience needed to catalyze enduring amendments to the fabric of governance.

Finally, the personal endorsement of constitutional values within one's daily life acts as a silent evangelism for the rights and liberties we so cherish. Living the tenets of the Constitution models an exemplary citizenship that upholds ideals not only in public fora but also within the privacy of home and hearth.

As the journey through these pages draws to a close, the path to change looms not as a distant horizon, but as an immediate course of action. Engaged citizenship doesn't passively inherit the future; it fervently co-creates it. Each step on the path, each effort expended in the direction of change, reaffirms the collective commitment to a republic that holds true to its founding principles—a republic where rights, endowed by the Constitution, are safeguarded and celebrated with unwavering accord.

Reclaiming the Republic

As we stand today at the crossroads of our nation's future, the power to shape that future lies resoundingly with us, the people. The journey through this book has illuminated the paths where our rights have been obscured and our liberties diminished. But the pages of history shine with the proof of what can be achieved when citizens unite in the defense of their freedoms.

Our founding document, the Constitution, was not set in stone but was crafted to adapt and thrive with the generations. Yet as we have seen, the true strength of the Constitution is only as formidable as the people's will to enforce it.

The First Amendment set the stage for a society where ideas could flourish without fear of retribution. The guarantees of free speech faced challenges, but where there is censorship, there is also the relentless voice of the collective, ready to reclaim that right.

The Second Amendment has spurred much debate, yet beyond the dissension lies a principle that we are all responsible for protecting our safety and sovereignty. We've grappled with how this right fits into our modern society, and it falls on us to navigate these waters with diligence and respect for the diversity of opinion.

The battles over privacy and property, the essence of the Third and Fourth Amendments, rage quietly in the halls of data centers and courtrooms. Technology has outpaced law, and we must catch up. Vigilance in protecting our personal space is a testament to our commitment to liberty itself.

The Fifth Amendment's call for due process echoes in the stories of those wrongly accused. The justice we seek for them is the justice we secure for ourselves.

The Sixth Amendment promised a fair trial, a right threatened by delays and obscurities. Reclaiming the Republic means insisting that transparency and speed are not mutually exclusive in our courts.

With the Seventh and Eighth Amendments under scrutiny, civil litigation and penal fairness stand as pillars that uphold the dignity of our system. Excessive punishments and overlooked rights within the legal process remind us that justice must not only be done but must be seen to be done.

Addressing the quieter Ninth and Tenth Amendments, we reaffirm the essence of our rights - those listed and those beyond the written word. Federal overreach clashes with the autonomy the framers vested in states and citizens - autonomy that still pulses at the heart of the Republic.

The War on Terror has tested the resilience of our Constitution, challenging us to balance security with freedom. Our response to this challenge will define the liberties of future generations.

The Judicial Branch was designed as the guardian of the Constitution, yet its potential for activism or restraint guides our nation's legal compass. It remains our call to ensure that compass points true north, towards justice and equality.

Presidential authority has its place, but the boundaries of executive power must be observed. When presidents push the limits, they challenge us to push back with the force of constitutional checks and balances.

Congress holds the key to our legislative future, but it has been known to lock out the very people it represents. Lawmaking must serve liberty, not restrict it, and every citizen has the right to hold their representatives accountable to that endowment.

Our Constitutional Amendments are more than historical footnotes; they are active directives that can strengthen the structure of our democracy when recognized and revered in contemporary society.

Yes, it is a complex and daunting task to reclaim the Republic which we have inherited. But the blueprint for such an undertaking has been written within the chapters of our collective past—teaching us that vigilance and proactive engagement are mandatory for the preservation of our Constitutional governance.

In this moment, an active, informed citizenry seems not just ideal but imperative. The Republic, as it stands, needs its citizens more than ever. The call to action is clear: education, participation, and unwavering commitment to the principles of freedom are the keystones of reclaiming the Republic we cherish.

Let this not be the end of our journey but the beginning of a renewed pledge to uphold and defend the principles that make our nation strong. Let us move forward with the courage to question, the strength to act, and the resolve to protect the beacon of liberty that is the United States of America.

Appendix A: Resources for Further Study

Empowerment begins with knowledge, and it's no different when it pertains to safeguarding our Constitutional rights. Unearth a deeper comprehension and get involved; the time is now to uphold the sacred promise of liberty.

A. Text of the United States Constitution

Knowledge starts at the source. The Constitution of the United States is our founding framework—it's essential to understand its words to grasp its power. Critical analysis begins with the foundational text itself:

- National Archives - *Charters of Freedom: A New World Is At Hand*

- Library of Congress - *Constitution Annotated*: In-depth study and interpretation of the American Constitution.

B. Landmark Supreme Court Cases

Supreme Court decisions shape our interpretation of the Constitution and our understanding of rights. Get acquainted with cases that have altered the judicial landscape:

1. *Marbury v. Madison*: Establishing judicial review.

2. *Brown v. Board of Education*: Ending racial segregation in schools.

3. *Roe v. Wade*: Rights to privacy and reproductive freedom.

4. *United States v. Nixon*: Limiting executive privilege.

5. *Obergefell v. Hodges*: Addressing marriage equality.

C. Advocacy Groups and Educational Organizations

Join forces with groups dedicated to maintaining and progressing the core values enshrined in our Constitution. Engage, educate, and advocate:

- **American Civil Liberties Union (ACLU)**: Promoting civil liberties and rights.

- **Institute for Justice**: Champions of limited government and individual liberties.

- **Educational Foundations**: Providing resources for constitutional education.

- **National Constitution Center**: Nonpartisan resources embracing the narrative of "We the People".

Chart the course towards a well-defended democracy. Understand the tools that lay before you and harness the power of participation. When the people are informed, the pillars of our Republic stand firm—undeterred by encroaching powers and rooted deeply in constitutional venerance.

A. Text of the United States Constitution

As we delve into the written words that frame the foundational liberties of this republic, we empower ourselves to reclaim the rights that were brilliantly encapsulated in the text of the United States Constitution. The Constitution isn't just archaic text; it is an enduring manifesto of freedom that breathes life into every letter, scribed with the intent to protect generations from government overreach.

The Constitution holds an intricate balance of power, structured to prevent any one branch from overtaking the others. It is a document of limitations and affirmations that says as much about what government cannot do as what it can. At its very beginning, the Preamble sets the stage for a government 'of the people, by the people, for the people'.

Article I vests all legislative powers in Congress, demarcating the scope of federal authority. It delineates the powers of the Senate and the House of Representatives, while also placing crucial restrictions on the laws they may pass. This intricate system of checks and balances is designed to maintain liberty as the legislature crafts laws.

Article II outlines the executive power, placing it in the hands of a President. This individual is entrusted with the leadership of the nation, yet is also restrained by the Constitution to prevent a monarchy or dictatorship. The Article defines procedures for election, powers and duties, and conditions for removal, ensuring that executive authority can be checked by the people and other branches. It ensures that power is both entrusted to lead and limited to protect.

Article III establishes the judiciary as an independent arbiter of the law, setting forth the powers of the Supreme Court and other federal courts. It grants the power to interpret the law and to deliver justice that should be unswayed by politics and pressures. Furthermore, the Constitution ensures that judges and justices serve for life, therefore theoretically protecting them from the whims of transient political climates.

Articles IV through VI cover the states' powers, the process for amendments, and the supremacy of the Constitution, respectively. They provide a framework for a unified nation, respecting the sovereignty of states while ensuring that the federal Constitution is the ultimate law of the land. This creates a robust structure that defends against both tyranny and fragmentation.

The Bill of Rights, consisting of the first ten amendments, explicitly outlines individual liberties and restraints on government power. It assures freedom of speech, religious practice, assembly, and the press—an impassioned declaration that these rights are intrinsic and unalienable. It affirms the right to bear arms, protecting citizens' ability to defend themselves and their autonomy from potential tyranny.

Additional amendments, from the 11th to the 27th, were ratified to refine and expand upon the original text, encompassing a broad range of issues including civil rights, voting rights, and the balance of powers within the federal government. Each one reflects an evolving understanding of liberty and justice as they extend protections to all citizens and adapt to the nation's growth.

What must be grasped is that every article and amendment enforces the notion that freedom is not a mere concept, but a concrete pillar that sustains the very idea of the United States. Governmental authority is derived from the consent of the governed, and when such authority steps beyond its bounds, it intrudes upon our constitutional safeguards.

The text's significance is unbounded by time; it's a living commitment to the preservation of liberty. When external pressures mount or internal fears rise, the Constitution's text is the bulwark that guards our freedoms. It is in this document where the battle lines are drawn, establishing the frontiers of freedom on which citizens can stand firm.

Understanding the Constitution means recognizing the delicate architecture of balance it creates. It is not a list of suggestions, but a set of principles cast in legal stone. Each word was chosen to echo through ages, to resonate with a citizenry prepared to demand adherence to its doctrines.

Reflecting on America's founding charter captures not just the spirit of a historical era, but ignites the essence of today's engagement in defending intrinsic rights. When you grasp its contents, you hold a roadmap to activism, a directive that prompts engagement, and a summons to challenge any infringements on people's sovereign rights.

Our journey through this Constitution must not be passive; it is not enough to know its words. One must also understand its meanings, its history, and its contemporary applications. This is how we fortify our guard against the erosion of rights. The text of the United States Constitution instills us with knowledge, and with it, the power to demand and uphold our freedoms.

The document's resilience is testament to its craft and foresight, and to the aspirations of those who penned it. It was designed not for the convenience of the government but for the protection of the governed. In every line and paragraph is an undying echo of the quest for liberty that enshrines our nation's perpetual fight against oppression and injustice.

With this understanding, we can wield the Constitution not as a mere shield but as a beacon, a rallying call that ensures rights are not only preserved but also revitalized and reinforced. In committing to the text of the Constitution, each citizen becomes a sentinel of their own rights and the rights of their fellow Americans. It inspires us not to falter, not to weary, but to continue the march toward a more perfect union.

B. Landmark Supreme Court Cases

In the spirit of sharpening our awareness of constitutional rights, a pivot towards the Supreme Court's palisades reveals the profound influence of certain landmark cases. These decisions serve as pillars that either bolster or erode the hallowed principles engraved in the Constitution. They're milestones, indicating the path taken in the nation's jurisprudential journey and their relevance to today's political climate must not be overlooked.

Among these, Marbury v. Madison (1803) stands as a testament to judicial review, the authority of our courts to nullify government acts contradicting the Constitution's essence. This doctrine, though not explicitly prescribed in the document, illustrates that interpretation can be as potent as the written word. Each word in the Constitution breathes life into our republic, and understanding its guardianship is paramount in preserving its fortitude.

Perhaps as famed as Marbury is Dred Scott v. Sandford (1857), a case that thickened the chains of slavery instead of breaking them. It delineated a time when the Court was blind to the very humanity the Constitution is meant to safeguard. The message is stark: remain vigilant, for the guardians of law can falter, leaving the spirit of the Constitution parched and in dire need of rejuvenation.

Brown v. Board of Education (1954) emerged as the North Star leading the nation out of the darkness of segregation. It serves as a lodestar reminding us of our capacity for growth, urging us to remain relentless in our pursuit of justice. This ruling transformed the educational terrains, setting a precedent that equal protection under the law must be more than a hollow promise.

Roe v. Wade (1973) brought attention to the shadows where personal autonomy clashes with moral and political currents. Regardless of the side one supports, the ramifications of this verdict touch the core of individual liberty. It heralds the Court's role in navigating the murky waters between the private lives of citizens and state intervention.

The contentious battle within The United States v. Nixon (1974) tethered the executive branch to answerability, affirming no individual is above the law. The ruling exemplifies the need for balance among the branches of government, a symphony of powers that must harmonize to protect constitutional ethos.

A groundbreaking stride in equality was achieved with Obergefell v. Hodges (2015), extending the sacred institution of marriage to all, irrespective of gender. It draws from the Constitution's reservoirs of liberty and equality, reinforcing the spirit of inclusivity that the document epitomizes. It compels us to acknowledge the evolving understanding of rights bound in history yet unfettered by it.

Citizens United v. Federal Election Commission (2010), however, stirs a more contentious debate on the First Amendment, with its expansive interpretation of freedom of speech in the context of political spending. This case broadens the discourse on the influence of wealth in politics, challenging citizens to consider whether their voices are muted by the sounds of expensive megaphones.

District of Columbia v. Heller (2008) and McDonald v. City of Chicago (2010) further illuminate the ever-present tensions surrounding the Second Amendment. These decisions affirm an individual's right to bear arms while also beckoning us to ponder the balance between rights and responsibilities in a society grappling with gun violence.

With the digital siege tightening around the concept of privacy, cases such as Carpenter v. United States (2018) signal the Court's awareness of technology's impact on Fourth Amendment protections. The preservation of personal privacy in the digital age is a modern challenge, cementing the role of constitutional law as a living entity, evolving alongside humankind's advancements.

These momentous cases serve not only as guideposts but also as watchtowers, reminding us of past victories, losses, and ongoing battles. Each is a stepping stone to heightened understanding and a call to engage with the judicial processes that shape the societal landscape. With this knowledge, individuals can strive to keep the torch of liberty ablaze.

This nexus of legal precedents links the past, present, and future. It accentuates the power embedded in the people when they are armored with knowledge and emboldened to demand that their rights not be impinged upon by the moment's whims.

True, these twilight struggles betwixt the pillars of power sometimes obscure the stars of our Constitution. Yet, in this uncertainty, a citizen armed with knowledge becomes not just a spectator but a participant in the great American experiment. We mustn't cast ourselves solely in the role of listeners to history's narrative, but as writers of the continuing chronicle of our time.

Embracing the essence of these cases embeds within us a deeper understanding of the Constitution's role in daily life. It enables us to champion the cause of freedom with vigor and defend against the creeping intrusions that threaten the framework of our liberties. For in the grand drama of governance, justice is not a mere abstraction; it is the very concrete plinth of civilization.

This excursion through landmark Supreme Court cases isn't simply an academic exercise. It's the toolkit for keeping democracy alive, the compass for navigating the terrain of rights and the scales for balancing the power vested in the hands of the few against the freedoms deserving of the many. To preserve the Republic, the vigil of constitutional literacy and engagement is our perpetual charge.

The significance of these cases extends beyond our borders and echoes into eternity. They reverberate as a reminder that the nation was conceived in ideals that must endure beyond the immediacy of current events. We stand on hallowed ground, watered with the wisdom and missteps of those who stood before the Court. May we draw from their sagas the strength to stand firm for the rights our Constitution enshrines.

C. Advocacy Groups and Educational Organizations

The lifeblood of any thriving democracy pulses through the veins of its informed citizens and the organizations that advocate for their rights. Recognizing the erosions of constitutional liberties is not merely about individual acknowledgment—it's about collective action and education. Across the nation, a network of advocacy groups and educational organizations operates with a clear mandate: to halt the relentless infringement upon rights guaranteed by the Constitution and to empower citizens through knowledge and proactive involvement.

These entities are not mere bystanders. They are the frontline defenders of liberty, engaging in legal battles, fostering public discourse, and disseminating critical information. Their work can often feel like an uphill struggle against waves of legislative and executive excesses that consistently test the boundaries of power. Yet, their resolve is unwavering, and their strategies are manifold.

Take for example the advocacy groups that focus on First Amendment rights. Their task is to ensure that free speech is not just a lofty idea enshrined in centuries-old parchment but a tangible, living right that is afforded to everyone. It's a daily commitment to push back against censorship and to champion the voices that would otherwise be silenced. These organizations provide resources, offer legal defense, and challenge laws that encroach upon freedom of expression.

Similarly, there are dedicated collectives combating the overreaches threatening the Second Amendment. Supporters are educated on responsible gun ownership while also advocating against legislation that infringes upon the right to bear arms without due balancing of the public safety considerations that also underpin constitutional interpretation.

Highlighting a less visible yet equally vital front, educational institutions play a key role in nurturing a deep-seated understanding of constitutional values. From workshops to seminars, from debates to publication of scholarly articles—their work aims to kindle a passion for civic responsibility and to toughen the intellectual armor of citizens against constitutional infringements.

These organizations know that knowledge is a powerful antidote to fear and a shield against tyranny. In a nation where laws and policies are frequently complex and opaque, they strive to demystify legal jargon, ensuring that the ordinary person understands how and when their rights are being compromised.

Moreover, the fusion of advocacy work with technological advances has opened new frontiers. Digital platforms are becoming potent tools in the hands of advocacy groups. Online campaigns, informative websites, and social media movements have immense power to sway public opinion and drive action at a scale that was previously inconceivable.

One cannot discuss educational organizations without applauding their tireless efforts in equipping the next generation with the knowledge of constitutional history and law. These entities foster critical thinking and empower youth with the capabilities to scrutinize government actions through the lens of constitutional protections.

When the smoke of legal and political battles clears, what often tips the scale is the grassroots support facilitated by these groups. They're able to amplify concerns, craft narratives, and mobilize masses in favor of protective measures for rights enshrined in the Constitution. This is the power of unity – an empowered public standing as one for the preservation of their rights.

Furthermore, these organizations contribute significantly to shaping policy by providing expert testimony in legislative hearings, submitting amicus briefs in judicial proceedings, and offering their extensive knowledge base to inform lawmakers and the judiciary alike.

Yet, advocacy and educational groups face their own challenges. Funding, political backlash, and public apathy can hinder their operations. It's in surmounting these hurdles that their true strength is proven – each obstacle is an opportunity to refine their approach, to innovate, and to reaffirm their commitment to constitutional governance.

Importantly, the success of these organizations isn't measured solely by courtroom victories or legislative changes. It's also found in the hearts and minds of people who've been inspired to stand for their rights, to raise their voice in town halls, and to cast their ballot with constitutional fidelity in mind.

The journey ahead remains fraught with challenges. Yet, it is also brimming with opportunities—for engagement, for education, and for inspiring a nationwide dialogue on constitutional rights. In a world that appears divided on many fronts, it is the relentless pursuit of these organizations to find common ground in the defense of liberties that unites us.

As we move forward, let us take a moment to appreciate the invaluable contribution of these stalwart guardians of our Constitution. Without their vigilance, without their voices, and without their visions for an enlightened populace, the narrative of freedom might have taken a different, darker turn.

Conclusively, this section underscores the pivotal role of advocacy groups and educational organizations in the preservation of our constitutional rights. The collective effort towards safeguarding the backbone of America's democracy is an evergreen testament to the power inherent in an informed, engaged, and active citizenry.